Savills
A Family and a Firm
1652—1977

By the same author

The Housing Act 1935 (1936, with T. J. Sophian)
Meet the Prisoner (1939)
The Child and the Magistrate (1942, 1950, 1965)
British Juvenile Courts (1948)
Which Is the Justice? (1969)
The Juvenile Court – 1970 Onward (1970)
Nothing But the Truth (1971, 1975)
The Incompleat Surveyor (1973)
The Modern Juvenile Court (1975, with P. M. Austin)

THE AUTHOR'S ROYALTIES ON THE SALE
OF THIS BOOK HAVE BEEN GIVEN TO THE
ROYAL INSTITUTION OF CHARTERED SURVEYORS'
BENEVOLENT FUND

JONATHAN SAVILL
1789–1849
'architect, builder, land agent and surveyor'

SAVILLS
A Family and a Firm
1652–1977

John A. F. Watson CBE, PPRICS

HUTCHINSON BENHAM, LONDON

Hutchinson Benham Ltd
3 Fitzroy Square, London W1P 6JD

An imprint of the Hutchinson Group

London Melbourne Sydney Auckland
Wellington Johannesburg and agencies
throughout the world

First published 1977
© John Watson 1977

Set in Monotype Bembo

Printed in Great Britain by The Anchor Press Ltd
and bound by Wm Brendon & Son Ltd
both of Tiptree, Essex

ISBN 0 09 129590 4

TO JACQUELINE
in memory of her father

Contents

Introduction   13

1   Early generations   15
    Henry and Elizabeth Savill (Gen. I, m. 1652) – the
    Dunmow Flitch – social discrimination – White Roothing
    – Jonathan Savill, master-bricklayer (Gen. V, 1758–1846)
    – Chigwell and a famous school – Jonathan Savill,
    'architect, builder, land agent and surveyor' (Gen. VI,
    1789–1849) – evolution of the valuer – a remarkable wife
    – Shaw Savill Line

2   Alfred Savill: a business and a practice   31
    Alfred Savill, 'land agent, surveyor and auctioneer'
    (Gen. VII, 1829–1905) – a London office – 'Savill and
    Son'– an office letter book – Mr Christie's water closet –
    professional practice – tithe, turnips and tithe rent-charge
    – repeal of the Corn Laws – Alfred's agencies – principles
    of estate management

3   New railways and an old forest   47
    Alfred Savill and the new railways – the Rocket –
    landowners and how they were compensated – Royal
    Forest of Waltham (Epping Forest), its history, enclosures
    and dedication – Alfred and the manorial lords – 'Alfred
    Savill and Sons' – Chigwell Hall – Alfred's death (1905)
    – a personal note

CONTENTS

4 Edwin Savill *v.* Lloyd George   60

*Three Savill brothers: Alfred (Gen. VIII, 1854–1928),
Edwin (1868–1947), Norman (1874–1945) – state of the
countryside – and of the towns – David Lloyd George and
his 'People's Budget'* – Edwin Savill and the Land Union
– the 'single-taxer' – The Land Report *and* The Land
Retort

5 Family interlude   74

*Three more Savill brothers: Lydall (Gen. IX,
1894–1940), Eric (b. 1895), Alfred Cecil (1897–1943) –
the Kemps – halcyon days in The Wilderness – King
Edward the peacemaker – memories of an early
twentieth-century upbringing – Blériot – Scott in the
Antarctic – the* Titanic *– gathering clouds – Savills at the
Front in the First World War*

6 1914–18: 'War to end Wars'   87

*Maintaining a practice – London managements – the
Company of Leathersellers – leasehold enfranchisement –
on valuers and valuing – Edwin Savill at the Home Front
– zeppelins – commandeering and compensation – war
damage and compensation for that – rent restrictions –
intensive food production*

7 Professional interlude   100

*Veterans of the staff – George Eve (1879–1959) – Daisy,
the underbidder – Sir Edwin Savill, President of the
Surveyors' Institution, 1924 – changes in the firm –
surprising effect of a half-bottle of port – Sir Eric Savill
and the Savill Garden in Windsor Great Park*

8 Between the wars   115

*Norman Savill and his country managements – royalty
disillusioned – the Wimborne estates – Viscount*

8

*Wimborne and the Ritz Hotel – rates, rating and
ratepayers – town and country planning – depression in
the nineteen-thirties – royal abdication – gathering clouds
again – Corporal Hitler – meeting at Munich*

9   1939–45: Hitler's war   126

*'Dig for victory' – Munich breathing space – stimulus for
agriculture – evacuation and dispersal – requisitioning and
war damage, how the owners were compensated this time –
doodle bugs and rockets – Lydall's death (1940) – Peter
Laycock (b. 1910) – 'All wars are the same' – Alfred
Cecil's death (1943) – the inept angler*

10 Postwar chronicle   137

*Norman Savill's death (1945) – and Edwin's (1947) –
a personal note – John Loscombe Lydall Savill (Gen. X,
b. 1917) – first postwar Labour government –
Agriculture Act 1947 – Town and Country Planning
Act 1947 – coming of the New Towns – John Watson
(b. 1903) – Lands Tribunal – 'Battle of Crichel Down'*

11 This modern age   151

*Background of events – town planning again, mend and
make do – changes in the firm – Henry Edward Savill
(Gen. IX, b. 1929) – 'Savills' – a visit to head office –
Land Commission 1967 – Community Land Act 1975 –
Development Land Tax Act 1976 – property investment
today – institutions as investors – farming partnerships –
the indestructible asset*

Appendix: The Savills, a skeleton pedigree   166

Index   169

Illustrations

Frontispiece

JONATHAN SAVILL, 1789–1849, 'architect, builder, land agent and surveyor'

Between pages 80 and 81

MARIA SAVILL (*née* LYDALL), 1807–1894, 'builder employing twenty men'

ALFRED SAVILL, 1829–1905, of Chigwell Hall

ALFRED SAVILL, 1854–1928

SIR EDWIN SAVILL, OBE, 1868–1947, President of the Surveyors' Institution, 1924–5

Between pages 136 and 137

HENRY NORMAN SAVILL, 1874–1945

EDWIN LYDALL SAVILL, 1894–1940

LIEUT.-COL. ALFRED CECIL SAVILL, DSO, MC, 1897–1943

SIR ERIC HUMPHREY SAVILL, KCVO, CBE, MC, *b.* 1895

Introduction

The Savills are an ancient family who came to England soon after the Norman Conquest. The branch we are concerned with in this book have their roots deep down in the corn lands of north Essex.

The early generations were yeomen farmers and as the years went by nearly all of them prospered. Some grew rich, some became important figures in their respective spheres, a few became national figures. But most of them were just honest, hard-working men and women of above-average intelligence who were born, married, had children and died in the fullness of time.

The story of the Savills, and of the firm of surveyors that bears their name, is part of the history of the soil. That is the background against which I have tried to tell it. The pages to follow contain a lightsome commentary, often discursive, on some of the outstanding events during the relevant period, especially those which have affected the land – its ownership, its use, its management and its value. They begin with the marriage of Henry Savill at Great Dunmow in 1652, and end with the coming into force of the Development Land Tax Act of 1976. But it is in no sense a history book, still less a tapestry. I prefer to describe it as an irregular patchwork with the story of the Savills threaded through it and holding the bits together.

I have so many friends to thank for their help in writing it. They include members of the Savill family, besides partners, retired partners and senior members of the staff in the firm now called Savills. It is not possible to name them all, but the advice I have had from four of them has been especially valuable. Miss

13

Bridget Lakin, genealogist, is a great-grand-daughter of Ebenezer Savill (Gen. VII, 1830–1911). Sir William Addison FSA, historian, is also a verderer of Epping Forest. Sir Desmond Heap LLM is a past-president of both the Law Society and the Royal Institute of Town Planning. Mr Edward Smith FRICS until he retired in 1973 was Superintending Valuer of the Inland Revenue, Eastern Region.

Quotations from published works are acknowledged in the footnotes. In particular, *English Farming Past and Present* by Lord Ernle, *Chartered Surveyors, the Growth of a Profession* by F. M. L. Thompson, and *The Forest of Essex* by W. R. Fisher were prolific sources of information.

I wish to make it clear, however, that any opinions expressed in this book are my personal opinions, and that I alone am to blame for any errors or omissions in the text.

J.A.F.W.

Elmdon Old Vicarage
Saffron Walden
March, 1977

I

Early generations

*Henry and Elizabeth Savill (Gen: I, m. 1652) – the
Dunmow Flitch – social discrimination – White Roothing
– Jonathan Savill, master-bricklayer (Gen. V, 1758–
1846) – Chigwell and a famous school – Jonathan Savill,
'architect, builder, land agent and surveyor' (Gen. VI,
1789–1849) – evolution of the valuer – a remarkable
wife – Shaw Savill Line*

On 24 March 1652 Henry Savill,* bachelor of Little Easton,
married Elizabeth Swallow, spinster of Dunmow, in the church
of Saint Mary the Virgin at Church End, in the parish of Great
Dunmow, in the county of Essex. The pedigree of their descendants, whom this book concerns, covers ten generations (see page
166).

Great Dunmow ('Dommawa' in Domesday Book) is a market
town on the Roman Stane Street and overlooks the Chelmer
Valley. It is thirty-eight miles north-east of London and thirteen
miles from the county town of Chelmsford. The parish of Little
Easton marches with Great Dunmow on the north, and is off
the Saffron Walden road a mile or more before you reach Church
End. The first cottages are close to the junction, but the village
is straggling and Little Easton church containing the splendid
monuments of the Maynard family is at the far end of it. It is
not known where in the village Henry Savill lived; his ancestors
had probably lived in Dunmow or its neighbourhood for
generations. As the couple were married in Great Dunmow

---

*'Savil, Savill, Savile, Saville, Saveall, Savell, Sayvell, Seville – "John de
Sayville" (1246); "Stephen de Savile" (1277). . . . Perhaps from Sauuille,
Ardennes and Vosges; or from Sainville, Eure-et-Loire'. Reaney, *Dictionary
of British Surnames.*

church, it is reasonable to assume that the Swallow family lived in the town. We shall refer to Henry and Elizabeth as 'Generation I'.

They were married in troublous times. The year of Henry Savill's birth is uncertain, but both he and Elizabeth had been brought up during the Civil Wars. The Second Civil War had broken out in 1648. On 30 January 1649, some three years before their marriage, King Charles I had been beheaded in Whitehall. Since then, Cromwell, intent on subduing Ireland, had massacred the garrisons of Drogheda and Wexford before leaving the finish of that campaign to his son-in-law, Ireton; had successfully invaded the Scots; and by winning the Battle of Worcester (3 September 1651) had completed his conquest of Britain.

There is no means of knowing how much the inhabitants of a small town like Great Dunmow had been affected by these cataclysmic events. It is likely, however, that the broad story of what was going on had filtered through, particularly as local families had been prominent in national affairs on both sides. Thus Sir John Bramston of Roxwell (d. 1654), formerly Chief Justice of the King's Bench, was a Royalist. Sir Hugh Masham of High Laver (d. 1656), who married a Barrington, was related to Cromwell and supported his cause; he had been imprisoned for refusing to lend money to the King – 'and milady too!' Cromwell himself, in 1620, had married Frances, daughter of Sir James Bourchier who had an estate at Felsted; all their four sons were educated at Felsted School.

It is unlikely that Little Easton has changed much over the years. This part of the county is pleasantly undulating, and the main difference is that in the seventeenth century there were smaller fields and certainly more trees than now; Dunmow is in the clay belt and was formerly dense forest. If Henry and Elizabeth could return, they would have no difficulty in recognizing Dunmow and the surrounding countryside with its fine half-timbered houses. Two important roads, one from London to the south-west and the other from Cambridge to the north, converge on the centre of the town opposite The Saracen's Head. And though many of the thatched roofs and plastered fronts of the town houses with their quaint pargeting have long ago been replaced by tiles and red brick, the High Street still pursues the same winding course until it leaves the town behind and leads on to Chelmsford.

The hamlet of Church End is north of the town. The fact that there was once a Saxon church here is evidence that this was the original Dunmow; the present town developed on the main road for purposes of trade. The church of Saint Mary the Virgin, built about the middle of the fourteenth century, is a superb example of the English Decorated period. The west tower, the clerestory and a splendidly embattled porch were added a century later. One of the earliest features is a thirteenth-century archway, supported by slender columns, enclosing the inner doorway of the porch which leads into the south aisle. Henry and Elizabeth would have passed under it after their wedding; and surely in the minds of the young couple, as they crossed the little church-yard, was the story of the ancient custom that has made this Essex town world-famous – the custom of the Dunmow Flitch.

Its origin is lost in antiquity. Francis Steer, an Essex archivist and author of a book on the subject,* thinks the custom may have dated from Norman times or possibly Saxon. There was an Augustinian priory, later to become a secular manor, in the village of Little Dunmow about two miles east of Great Dunmow. The custom was for the prior and his canons to award a flitch of bacon to any couple who could establish on oath that neither had repented their marriage for a year and a day. It is mentioned by Chaucer (c. 1340–1400) in *The Miller's Tale*. In 1445 the author of *Reliquiae Antiquae*, deploring the low standards of contemporary morals, regretted that he could

> Fynd no man now that wille enquere
> The parfyte wais unto Dunmow;
> For they repent hem within a yere,
> And may within a weke, and souner, men trou. . . .

* The History of the Dunmow Flitch Ceremony, 1951.

The first recorded award of the flitch was to Richard Wright, a yeoman, in 1445; his wife is not mentioned! The last award by the Court Baron was to Thomas and Ann Shakeshaft in 1771. Thereafter the then lord of the manor, successor in title to the prior and his canons, declined to admit claims (and presumably provide the flitch) and the custom lapsed. There was nothing frivolous about the ceremony in early days and the oath was solemn. In a period when so many unmarried men and women cohabitated, it was possibly devised as a reminder of the importance and sanctity of marriage. As to the bacon, the sow and her farrow have been emblems of fertility since Roman times, and a flitch of bacon was kept hanging in the temple of the appropriate deity during the reign of Augustus.

Since 1771, the custom has been revived privately in Great Dunmow from time to time. But the ceremony, with questionable embellishments, has degenerated into no more than entertainment for the masses who attend or watch it on television.

When Henry Savill and his bride came out into the early spring sunshine, hopeful of many years of happiness, is it not likely that they planned one day to claim the award? There is no record of their having done so, but their marriage was blessed with fertility without the stimulus of a side of bacon. They had five sons and four daughters; two of the sons lived to be over seventy, which was a great age in that period. Lambert Savill (Gen. II, 2nd son) was born in 1656 and married for the second time in 1728. Unhappily he died the following year.

All the second generation of Savills were born in the parish of Little Easton and most of them died there. There is little doubt that like their forbears they all worked on the land, though Lambert was a wheelwright as well as a farmer. Henry Savill's third son, Jonathan Savill (Gen. II, 1660–1729), from whom the Savills we are concerned with are descended, is described as a yeoman. So is his son, Daniel Savill (Gen. III, 1698–1755). It may be of interest to record briefly what these and kindred descriptions meant.

Agricultural labourers were the lowest rung of the rural ladder, both socially and economically. *The Oxford English Dictionary* defines a labourer as 'one who does work requiring chiefly bodily strength and aptitude and little skill or training, and distinguished e.g. from an artisan'. An agricultural, or farm, labourer was a man who worked on someone else's land for a wage.

Next on the social and economic ladder came the farmers and husbandmen, who cultivated the soil as their means of livelihood. There does not seem to have been much difference between the two; but Cobbett (1762–1835) makes this distinction between them and yeomen: 'Those who rent . . . are, properly speaking, farmers. Those who till their own land are yeomen; and when I was a boy, it was common practice to call the former farmers and the latter yeomen farmers.'* And we are told by Canon J. C. Atkinson (1814–1900) that 'down to the first half of the seventeenth century the appellation husbandman still distinguished the man of the class below yeoman'.†

The yeoman, next rung up the ladder, was a man owning and farming a small landed estate and might be a person of substance. Thus Sir Thomas Smith in 1584: 'Yeoman: which worde now signifieth among us a man well at ease and having honestlie to live, and yet not a gentleman.'‡

A gentleman was a person described rather vaguely as 'of gentle birth'. He did not necessarily own land or have any connection with agriculture. An esquire (literally 'shield-bearer') was socially superior to a gentleman. Esquires included the younger sons of peers and their eldest sons, and the eldest sons of knights and their eldest sons. The appellation was also accorded to persons holding the Sovereign's commission – e.g. justices of the peace and leading counsel – and to certain persons by virtue of their office. Thus Samuel Pepys on 25 March 1660: 'There was [a letter] for me from Mr Blackburne, who with his own hand superscribes it to *S.P. Esqr.* of which, God knows, I was not a little proud.'

Rural Rides, 1830.
†*Forty years in a Moorland Parish*, 1891.
‡*Commonwealth of England*, vol. 1, 1584.

Those members of the early generations of Savills who cultivated their own land were copyholders as well as freeholders.
The manorial system of land tenure had been firmly established
in rural Essex since Norman times and is said to have evoved
from the Saxon system known as bondage; lands that werel not
held directly from the Crown were held from the lord of the
manor as an intermediary. The term 'copyholder', first employed
in the fourteenth century, derived from the fact that the occupier
had as his title a copy of the relevant entry in the manorial court
roll, wherein all changes of occupation ('admittances' and 'sur-
renders') were recorded.

A typical medieval manor was divided into four parts. First,
there was the demesne, including the manor house and ancillary
buildings occupied by the lord and his family. Second, there were
lands occupied by 'freemen' in return for military service to the
lord of the manor, or for rent in money or kind. Third, there
was 'unfree' land, sometimes known as the village farm, which
was occupied by various social grades of 'bondsmen'; the highest
were the 'villeins' and the lowest the 'serfs'. Fourth, around the
village and possibly extending a long way into the countryside,
were woodlands, rough pastures occupied in common, and
untilled waste lands. These early Savills were probably descended
from bondsmen, whose rank and the extent of whose holdings
on the manorial land were proportionate to the services they
rendered to the lord; and these in turn were measured by the
number of oxen the bondsman was able to contribute to the
plough-team working on the demesne.

We have seen that Jonathan Savill, yeoman (Gen. II, 1660–
1729), was the fourth son of Henry and Elizabeth. He had been
brought up with his brothers and sisters in Little Easton. They are
unlikely to have had any formal education. Their England was
before the England of Oliver Goldsmith and 'those good old
motherly dames, found in every village, who clutch together the
whole callow brood . . . and teach them their letters'. He married
by licence, on 18 March 1684 at Bishop's Stortford, a widow
named Grace Overill, daughter of Isaac Jarvis, yeoman, and they

lived in the village of White Roothing, one of a cluster of villages on the banks of the River Roding, a few miles south of Great Dunmow.

It is evident from his will that Jonathan was a yeoman farmer of substance. He left his daughter, Martha Felton, a house called Larks, where she lived with her husband, together with outhouses, barn, stable and a plot of arable land that went with them. To his grandson, Jonathan (Gen. IV, *b.* 1726), 'son of my son, Daniel' (Gen. III, 1698–1754), he left 'a close, late copyhold, now freehold, lying in White Roothing, about two acres'. To Daniel himself, executor, he left the sum of £220. To his wife, Grace, an annuity of £12 'and a feather bed and all belonging thereto, which is standing in the parlour'. One wonders what the bed was doing in the parlour until one notices that his will was dated 19 April 1729; he was buried at White Roothing five days later. The bed is likely to have been brought downstairs during his last illness and possibly he died in it.

Jonathan Savill (Gen. II, 1660–1729) and his wife had in all four sons and four daughters; we have seen already that the youngest of the sons, Daniel, was a yeoman like his father. Daniel was born in 1698 at White Roothing and married, at Leaden Roothing, Margaret Green; she was a grand-daughter of Isaac Green, a big farmer in the parish of Hatfield Broad Oak, a few miles to the west.

Daniel and Margaret Savill lived for a time at White Roothing, but in about 1730 they too moved to Hatfield Broad Oak. They had nine children – six sons and three daughters. Soon after the move they became Nonconformists; the third child, Elizabeth (Gen. IV, 1731–1762), was baptized at Hatfield Heath Independent Chapel and was buried at Hatfield Broad Oak. It would appear that all the sons worked on the land.

Daniel's eldest son, Jonathan, who inherited the two acres from his grandfather, had been born at White Roothing before the move. He married a girl called Sarah Speller of the same village and the young couple continued to live in it. A son and grandson of yeomen farmers, he is referred to in contemporary documents as 'Mr Jonathan' which implied some standing in the local community. His son, yet another Jonathan (Gen. V, 1758–1846), was clearly anxious to do the best he could for his branch of the Savills both socially and financially.

This third Jonathan Savill in the direct line, of whom we now treat, was an important member of the family. He was the second of eleven children all of whom were born in White Roothing. He married Mary Green, daughter of a well-to-do farmer who was probably related to the Greens of Hatfield Broad Oak. He and his family moved to Chigwell Row, which at that time was part of the parish of Chigwell, east of the great Waltham Forest and about fourteen miles from the centre of London. Jonathan was then 26 and described himself as a bricklayer; he lived in Chigwell for the rest of his life and was 88 when he died. His was the first generation of Savills one or more of whose members ceased to earn their living as farmers. A younger brother, Isaac Savill, also moved to Chigwell, became a bricklayer and probably worked under him. Another brother, named Daniel after his grandfather, became a victualler.

In the eighteenth century firms of building contractors, as we know them today, did not exist in country districts. The forerunners of the contractors were the master-masons who supervised the erection of such buildings as the stately mansions designed by distinguished architects for the nobility. But most of the new buildings in that period, and extensions to buildings, were the product of a collaboration between local tradesmen who had their own workshops and were financially independent of one another. 'Master-tradesman' implied not only a skilled craftsman, but an employer of labour. One of the most important of these was the master-bricklayer, who was responsible for drawing up the plans and marshalling the various trades. Jonathan Savill was a master-bricklayer and doubtless had bricklayers as well as unskilled labourers on his payroll.

Why did Jonathan Savill choose to go to Chigwell? An obvious reason is that he was ambitious and anxious to expand his business and make money; there was little prospect of that in such a remote village as White Roothing. Another likely reason was a concern for the education of his children.

The road from London to Chelmsford by way of Ongar passes through Chigwell, and even in those days must have carried a considerable volume of traffic. The metropolis, moreover, was already beginning to expand in that direction. Even so, it was essentially a country village and Dickens, who conceived most of *Barnaby Rudge* while staying at The King's Head, could still be lyrical about it. He wrote to John Forster:

Chigwell, my dear fellow, is the greatest place in the world, name your day for going, such a delicious old inn opposite the churchyard – such a lovely ride – such beautiful forest scenery – such an out of the way rural place. . . .

Samuel Harsnett, who rose to be Archbishop of York after holding the sees of Chichester and Norwich, had been vicar of Chigwell from 1599 to 1615. Thereafter he became Archdeacon of Essex, and in 1629 he returned to Chigwell to found and endow two free schools. One was the 'Latin School' and the other the 'English School'. The functions of the English School were transferred to a new elementary school established in about 1870, but the Latin School became one of the foremost grammar schools in that part of the country. Harsnett, a High Churchman, made it a condition that the master should be 'of sound religion, neither Papist nor Puritan . . . no Tippler, Haunter of Alehouses, no Puffer of Tobacco'. A further condition, that the master must avoid all 'Novelties and conceited Modern Writers', suggests that the founder, besides being a High Churchman, was what one day would become known as a High Tory. But Harsnett was also a humanitarian: he stipulated that no master in his school should strike a scholar on the head on pain of being fined forty shillings for each offence.

When in 1786 Jonathan Savill married and moved to Chigwell, Archbishop Harsnett's grammar school had been established for more than 150 years. What more likely than that a master-tradesman, born and brought up in the country, should have wanted to continue living in a country village: that he should have chosen a village which, though not yet a London suburb, was likely to ripen for development as the years passed; and that he should have chosen one which, in addition to those advantages, afforded him an exceptional opportunity to secure a good education for his sons – if not, in those days, for his daughters?

The eldest son, Jonathan (Gen. VI, 1789–1849), was baptized at Chigwell, so presumably he was born in the parish. It is evident from his later professional achievements that he had not only had a grammar-school education, but a very good one. Unfortunately, the register of *alumni* of Chigwell grammar school in his period in incomplete, but it is likely that he went there about the turn of the century. Later he sent his eldest son, Alfred Savill (Gen. VII, 1829–1905). Alfred in turn sent all his five sons, although three of them went to public schools afterwards.

On leaving school Jonathan went to work under, and later in partnership with, his father. The latter, judging from the not inconsiderable estate he left in 1846, soon became established as a local builder. He was content, however, to continue describing himself as a bricklayer and did so in a codicil shortly before he died. Not so his eldest son. The young man worked hard and prospered, and it was probably in the mid 1850s that he first described himself as 'architect, builder, land agent and surveyor'. He might have added 'valuer', in which capacity, as we shall see, he earned distinction.

There is no record of Jonathan's being apprenticed to an architect or receiving any professional training. Building was the mainstay of his business, and 'architect' probably implied no more than that he designed the houses he built, as do many modern speculative builders.

A 'land agent' today is a professional man who manages one or more country estates. He fixes rents, negotiates tenancies, collects the rents, sees to it that the tenants discharge their liability for repairs, and advises his clients on the multiplicity of considerations, statutory and otherwise, which in this modern age affect the landowner. If, moreover, he is in general practice,

as opposed to being a resident agent, he may buy and sell properties for clients on commission. In the early nineteenth century
the lawyers still enjoyed a monopoly of this work. The attorney-
steward, especially if in the service of an absentee landlord,
performed much more than purely legal duties like conveyancing.
He combined the functions of a modern land agent with the
responsibility for advising his employer on such matters as
investments and mortgages. Many of the attorneys, no doubt,
were conscientious men who put their employers' interests first.
There is evidence, however, that not a few betrayed their trusts
by accepting illicit commissions and bribes.

The surveyor-steward made his appearance about the end of
the eighteenth century. He does not seem to have been so successful in feathering his nest as some of the attorneys – possibly
because he had less opportunity for doing so. Sales of landed
property by auction were becoming fashionable; it is likely that
the land agents had their share and became valuers on the strength
of the knowledge they acquired. Others of the early auctioneers
were farmers. William Hussey of Honiton, farmer and butcher,
took to selling land by auction: he remained in business as a
butcher, but became what we should describe today as an estate
agent as well. While Nathaniel Kent, author of *Hints to Gentlemen
of Landed Property* (1775), opened an office in the City of London,
'where estates for purchase and sale are estimated, and calculations
of every denomination that can affect them are made upon terms
of moderation'.

Another class of persons who tended to become valuers and
estate agents were the land surveyors. The early surveyors had
been purely measurers and mappers. The Ordnance Survey did
not come into existence until about 1790 and at the outset was
mainly concerned with mapping for military purposes. Previously
all the county maps had been made, and many of them beautifully
executed, by cartographers such as Saxton, Norden and John
Speed. Estate maps for sales and lettings and for recording
boundaries were the handiwork of quite humble people instructed
by attorneys. Between 1790 and 1851 was the heyday of the

enclosures, and accurate mapping was vital to that exercise. A typical Act for enclosure entrusted the responsibility for the apportionment and valuation of the land to statutory commissioners, who were at pains to prevent the surveyors usurping their function. Inevitably, however, by virtue of what they learned while measuring and mapping, many surveyors of that period became valuers as well.

From the opening years of the nineteenth century, when Jonathan Savill (Gen. VI, *b.* 1789) left school and joined his father, until his own death in 1849, he was primarily a builder. But it is evident that his professional expertise, if only a side line, was recognized. A report and valuation which he made for the then Bishop of London in 1836 are still in existence. A piece of glebe land in Chigwell was required for the building of a new schoolroom. Jonathan Savill, 'land surveyor', was employed to value it for the vendors. He begins his report by reciting his instructions in 'an Instrument in writing under the hand of the Right Reverend Father in God Charles James by divine permission Lord Bishop of London'. Then he identifies the land in words and by reference to a map annexed to the document – and continues:

I the said Jonathan Savill did on the fifth day of December One thousand eight hundred and thirty six carefully survey the said piece or parcel of ground and measure the same and I do certify that the said piece or parcel of ground including the ditch surrounding the same contains exactly One Rood Thirty Six Poles and does not exceed that quantity and I am of opinion that the sum of Forty pounds is the value of the same reckoning the said land as freehold. . . .

The next step in the proceedings is an acknowledgement signed personally by the Bishop. There follows a further document signed by Savill containing an assurance that his report and valuation are correct –

. . . and I make this solemn declaration conscientiously believing the same to be true by virtue of the powers of an Act made and passed in the Fifth and Sixth years of the reign of His present Majesty intituled 'An Act to repeal an Act of the present session of Parliament intituled

"An Act for the more effectual abolition of Oaths and Affirmations taken and made in various departments of the State and to substitute declarations in lieu thereof and for the more entire suppression of voluntary and extra judicial Oaths and Affidavits and to make other provisions for the abolition of unnecessary oaths" '.

This further document is then witnessed by one of His Majesty's justices of the peace. To the modern reader these preliminaries to a simple transaction sound absurdly complicated, and one can only assume that the parties had plenty of time on their hands. One wonders how long it was before Parliament passed yet another Act intituled 'for the more effectual abolition of unnecessary declarations'.

Jonathan Savill was in his sixtieth year when he died in September 1849, only three years after his father, the bricklayer. He had been born into a family of yeomen farmers and country craftsmen, his grammar-school education had ended in his early teens, and a university had not been thought of. He had learned his job the hard way on the building site, in the workshop, later at an office desk. He prospered, and some may have described him as a 'self-made' man. But they would have been wrong; he was not entitled to that distinction. The man in the making was vastly indebted to the wonderful woman who was his second wife.

His first marriage had ended tragically. Ann Bellin, of Chigwell, was an elder sister of Samuel Bellin (1799–1893), the painter and engraver. She was about 25 at the date of the marriage and Jonathan was 30. Three years later they had a daughter whom they christened Mary Ann. Ann died of a 'decline' six months afterwards, and the child two months after her mother.

Jonathan Savill remained a widower for nearly three years. Then, in October 1826, he married again. Maria Lydall was a daughter of John Lydall of Uxmore House, Ipsden, in Oxfordshire. She had taken a post as a governess – one of the few jobs available in those far-off days to a young woman of gentle birth – and had come to stay at Chigwell vicarage; that is where they met. Jonathan Savill was now 37 and his bride only 19. Their marriage, at Nettlebed, was unpopular with her relations. For one thing there was the disparity in their ages. For another, which possibly weighed more heavily, in those days a daughter of a county family who had married into 'trade' was considered to have demeaned herself. Maria, in her old age, said she had never for one moment regretted doing so.

We are indebted to her descendants for pen-portraits. She was witty as well as intelligent, and a mistress of the quick retort. On one occasion, in Hyde Park, she was negotiating the low iron fence which divided the turf from the gravelled footpath – not a simple exercise in that period of long, trailing skirts. A policeman who happened to be passing was embarrassed: 'Madam, I think you should know that you are showing part of your leg.' She responded with a charming smile: 'Then take a really *good* look, Officer, you won't have another chance.'

It was characteristic that she maintained a close friendship with the Bellins, the family of her husband's first wife. Maria was a handsome woman judging from a portrait in oils by Samuel Bellin; there are also two attractive miniatures of her and Jonathan, painted soon after their marriage when she was scarcely more than a girl.

She is said to have had the gift of being able to get the very best out of people. 'Granny Savill', wrote one of her grandchildren, 'was a most remarkable woman, seen perhaps once in a lifetime and once only. I have never met anyone like her since.' An outstanding quality was the courtesy she showed everybody. She told her grand-daughter, then aged about 17, that she ought to be able to receive 'properly' anyone from the Queen herself down to the humblest of Her Majesty's subjects.

'But, Granny, if I had to receive the Queen, there'd be much more etiquette than if I had to receive, say, a gypsy woman?'

Her granny replied: 'More etiquette of course, my dear, but the *courtesy* would be the same.'

But there was more to Maria Savill than intelligence, a good presence and nice manners. She was also courageous and possessed what in that period was rarely found in a woman – a sound business sense. She and Jonathan had had ten children, six sons and four daughters. The eldest son, Alfred, was still only 19 when his father died. Ebenezer, Philip, Walter and Martin were 18, 17, 13 and 7 respectively; Walter and Martin were still at school. Sidney, the youngest, was a baby. And, to make things more difficult for their mother, Maria Lydall, 22 and the eldest, though mentally normal, was a dwarf.

Maria Savill, aged 42, had no doubt where her duty lay. It was to hold her husband's business together until one or other of her sons was old enough to take charge of it; see that the older boys found good jobs when they left school; ensure that the education of the younger children was not interrupted. The following extract from the census return for Chigwell, less than two years after Jonathan's death, affords a glimpse of how she was discharging it: 'HEAD OF FAMILY: Maria Savill, widow aged 44, builder employing 20 men'.

Young Alfred, aged 19, was his mother's main support. Ebenezer and Philip became successful brewers (Savill Brothers) and founded the family brewery at Stratford in East London. Walter perhaps was the most remarkable; although he was not concerned with building or surveying, no book touching on the Savill family would be complete without a short record of his achievements.

On 14 December 1850, a little more than a year after their father's death, Alfred received the following letter concerning his brother, Walter, who was not yet 15. It was from Mr Henry H. Willis at 3 Crosby Square in the City of London:

Mr Henry H. Willis' compliments to Mr Savill and begs to inform him that he will take his brother into his Office as Clerk, the answers to his enquiries being highly satisfactory....

Mr Willis was head of Messrs Willis, Gann and Company, an important firm of shipbrokers, who were in competition with the Albion Line to New Zealand. Walter Savill accepted the offer and entered its freight department on the following New Year's Day at a commencing salary of £20 a year. It was raised in 1853 to £50, plus a 'dinner contribution' (presumably equivalent to luncheon vouchers) of £15.

The head of the freight department was a brilliant and enterprising young man called Robert Ewart Shaw. A few years later, feeling he had been slighted by his principals, Shaw decided to start in business on his own account and persuaded Walter Savill to join him. Owing to shortage of capital they began in a small way as brokers, but were soon engaged in chartering vessels to carry cargo and emigrants to the new colony. In 1859 they attracted attention with a Liverpool ship, *Spray of the Ocean*, which did the voyage from London to Auckland in the unprecedented time of eighty-three days. Shortly afterwards they founded Shaw Savill, which after a merger became the famous Shaw Savill and Albion Line.

Maria Savill died in 1894 at the age of 86. Her four elder sons, grandsons of an Essex master-bricklayer, left between them nearly £2½ million. The fifth son, Martin, had considerable charm but was less successful in business in spite of having married the daughter of a Lord Mayor of London; he is said to have been extravagant and left very little. The sixth son, Sidney, died as a child. It is on record that three of the Savill brothers of that generation were known by their contemporaries in the City as 'Grab All' (Walter); 'Save All' (Alfred); 'Spend All' (Martin).

2

Alfred Savill: a business and a practice

Alfred Savill, 'land agent, surveyor and auctioneer'
(Gen. VII, 1829–1905) – a London office – 'Savill and
Son' – an office letter book – Mr Christie's water closet –
professional practice – tithe, turnips and tithe rent-charge –
repeal of the Corn Laws – Alfred's agencies – principles
of estate management

Chigwell and Chigwell Row, as we mentioned earlier, though rather straggling, were originally one parish. The village contained a number of substantial detached houses, each with its grounds, outbuildings and stabling, some of which still exist. Members of the Savill family occupied a number of these houses, and in a period when there was little public transport were doubtless happy to have their close relations as their neighbours. We have seen that Jonathan Savill (Gen. VI) died in 1849 and that Maria Savill, his widow, carried on the family business. In 1856 the eldest son, Alfred Savill married Eleanor Hallings, daughter of John Smith, a farmer of Chigwell, and set up house nearby.

It is unlikely that Maria had to control the business for long. Alfred had had an excellent grounding in all its departments and in 1855, when still only 26, he opened an office at 27 Rood Lane in the City of London. In the autumn of 1860 he complained to a firm of liverymen in Brentwood near his home that his mother had been overcharged: 'She keeps one only pony and chaise; . . . *my mother is not in any business.'**

Among the firm's few archives is an office letter book from the

---

*Author's italics.

spring of 1859 until the end of the following year. The other side of the correspondence is unfortunately missing; even so, the outgoing letters provide a glimpse of what the business then comprised and of the man who wrote them. A Mr Millington was chief clerk. Nearly all the letters are in Alfred's flowing longhand and are signed personally. When, however, Mr Millington writes a letter, it is signed by that gentleman on behalf of 'Savill and Son'. The inference is that Mr Millington was an employee of long standing and that 'Savill' was Jonathan (Gen. VI, 1789–1849), Alfred's father.

There were two sides to the business – a builder's business and a professional business – and the former was the more extensive and the more profitable. But increasingly, as the years passed, Alfred conducted his professional practice as 'land agent, surveyor and auctioneer' from his office in the City of London. The builder's business remained centred on Chigwell, and as late as 1868, on the birth certificate of his third son, Edwin (Gen. VIII, 1868–1947), he was content to describe himself as 'builder'. Later in life, when Alfred had become one of the most distinguished surveyors of his day, the builder's business was disposed of. He was also a farmer. That was in the Savill blood and at one time, probably for clients as well as for himself, he was farming between 400 and 500 acres.

Alfred Savill was a builder of houses, villas, cottages, tenements – each no doubt with 'the usual offices'. He was also employed as a builder by the railway company which served the Essex suburbs and was extending eastward. In 1859 he tendered for the construction of a new station at Shalford Bridge, and he was already engaged in building a refreshment room at Loughton. In connection with the latter, he had been instructed to fence an adjoining field that had been acquired by the company as a 'pleasure ground for passengers'; one wonders what use the passengers made of it, and how long they had to disport themselves between the missing of one train and the arrival of the next.

His building department also had a heavy programme of repairs. But Savill was more than a jobbing builder and had a number of useful contracts. They included the repair of Chigwell Grammar School, the national schools at Loughton and Theydon Bois, and several mansions in the neighbourhood. He was a careful estimator and, like most builders, wary of extras; they were apt to delay the completion of the job and lead to disputes over payment. Once an estimate had been accepted, he supervised the work personally almost to the last detail. His investigation of the blockage of Mr Christie's water closet was typical.

In the middle of the nineteenth century a water closet *inside* a country house was still a rarity, and one seldom encountered a bathroom. Indoor sanitation was less in demand than conservatories – perhaps because the latter, being conspicuous, were more likely to impress the neighbours. Savill appears to have been an expert in conservatories and was building several. One suspects that in those days a conservatory was a status symbol, a heated swimming pool being its modern equivalent.

Whether or not Mr Christie had a conservatory, he possessed at least one water closet. It was, however, outside the house and its construction was primitive. The pan, which presumably discharged into a cess pit, was flushed from an overhead cistern operated by a valve. The cistern, open to the sky, was replenished by rain water mainly from the gutters around the roof of the house. Mr Savill's letter, dated January 1860, states the problem and how it was solved:

With reference to the repairs to the W. Closet, it was difficult to ascertain the cause of the stoppage. We first thought it was the leaves and then put a cover to the cistern that did not succeed. After this we found that very small pieces of mortar washed away from the tiles on the roofs [had] got into the cistern. We then put a strainer on the water spout from the roof, but finding the spout quite decayed we feel it needs a new one as stated in your letter.

So Mr Christie had cause for satisfaction under two heads: first, the prospect of getting his 'toilet' back into use; second, that in identifying that broken old water spout as being part of the

B   33

trouble (as he had told Mr Savill in the first place) he had been right.

Savill's professional practice already included some estate management – albeit the estates were very small compared with some he managed later. In 1859 we find him advising the lords of the manors of Chigwell and West Hatch on the amounts due to them in fines and the compensation payable on enfranchisement. He also conceives it his duty (as should every good estate agent) to warn his employer against a course of action that might injure his reputation. A letter to another manorial lord contained the following passage:

We must not go too fast about the grants. You, I think, know that you are the only lord that has enclosed and granted wastes in this parish; on the other manors they are opposed.

But all Savill's clients were not manorial. In the same year the winding up of the estate of the late Reverend George Perry on the instructions of the executors was giving him a lot of trouble. He also had many clients who, though they may have owned the houses they lived in, would scarcely have been described as landowners. He valued their houses for sale or letting, and sold them privately or at auction. He assessed dilapidations and made frequent inspections to ensure that the outgoing tenants were doing the work properly. He also collected rents, and a tenant who defaulted without good cause, or failed to honour an undertaking, could expect short shrift. The following was written to a lady who had mortgaged her jewellery and wanted to redeem it before paying her arrears:

In reply to your letter . . . I beg to say that I cannot give you further time for the payment you promised last month for rent. I do not understand that it can make any difference whether you redeem your jewels now or in a month's time. I have called upon you several times and now hope you will pay the sum arranged without further delay.

In 1860 he was instructed by Mr William Whitaker Maitland of Loughton Hall, some two and a half miles north-west of

Chigwell, to act for him and the tenant farmers in connection with a proposed extension of the Eastern Counties Railway to Epping. The line was to cross the Loughton Hall estate and they were entitled to compensation. This is unlikely to have been Alfred Savill's first job arising out of the construction of the new railways, and it was certainly not the last. There were three great railway 'booms' in his lifetime. The first was from 1835 to 1837; the second from 1844 to 1847; the third in the 1860s when he was in his prime. It is on record that the third boom brought him much work as a valuer, a branch of his practice that we shall return to presently.

He had not come on the scene early enough to take any material part in the assessment of tithe rent-charge under the provisions of the Tithe Commutation Act of 1836. Commutation of tithe was only one factor, but an important one, in the recovery from the depression that had beset the agricultural industry since the early years of the century. Savill, however, in building up his professional practice, undoubtedly benefited by the results of it.

Historically, tithe was a payment in kind by a parishioner of a tenth part of the produce of his land to the person or persons who ministered to his spiritual welfare. After the dissolution of the monasteries by Henry VIII, some of the 'rectories' were re-granted by the Crown to the incumbents of Church of England benefices. Others went to private individuals who were known, and are still known, as lay rectors. As years went by, the whole business of the levying and payment of tithe had become increasingly unpopular, and some of the farmers made the collection of tithe as difficult as possible. 'A Hampshire farmer gave notice to the tithe-owner that he was about to draw a field of turnips. When the tithe-owner's servants, horses and waggons had come on to the land, the farmer drew ten turnips, gave one to the tithing man, and said he would let his master know when he would draw any more.'*

It is not surprising that for a long time there had been a practice

---

*Lord Ernle, *English Farming, Past and Present*, 6th edition, 1961.

by tithe-owners, especially if clergymen, to come to terms with their tithe-payers and convert the tithes into monetary payments. Eventually it became recognized, by Whigs and Tories alike, that the continuance of the existing system was militating powerfully against agricultural advancement and that some drastic revision of the law was called for.

The Tithe Commutation Act 1836 made the commutation of tithe compulsory. It provided for the fixing of an annual payment which would fluctuate with the purchasing power of money and equate the value of titheable produce to the current cost of living. The first step was to convert the total value (e.g. in bushels of corn) of tithe paid by all the parishioners into a total parochial rent-charge; the second to apportion the rent-charge among the titheable properties, all of which had to be clearly marked on a local tithe map. The Act brought a lot of work to surveyors. A land surveyor was required to survey and map the ground; a valuer, who might be the same person, to make the valuations and apportionments. Jonathan Savill, 'architect, builder, land agent and surveyor', is likely to have had a hand in both.

One consequence of the statutory commutation of tithe had been a greater demand for agricultural land as an investment. But there had been other reasons for that. The industrial revolution had had the effect of stimulating agriculture; the cultivation of the soil for the production of food could no longer be restricted to meeting the needs of a scattered and mainly rural population. The advent of steam power was affording an ever-increasing fillip to trade. Joint-stock banks were giving financial assistance to farmers. The importance of specializing in such matters as the improvement of our breeds of livestock had become recognized.

But there was another factor which made some people think differently. In spite of all this progress, their outlook was gloomy and they viewed the future of our agricultural industry, and the demand for land that might be expected to flow from it, with foreboding.

In 1849, the year of Jonathan Savill's death, the Corn Laws were finally repealed. Many agriculturists were fearful of the consequences. They 'argued, and no doubt conscientiously believed, that, if corn in any quantity were brought into the country from abroad, home-prices would cease to yield reasonable profits; that agricultural land would be forced out of cultivation; that rents and wages would fall; that rural employment would diminish; that the virility of the nation would be impaired by the influx into the towns and the depopulation of country districts'.*

The Corn Laws had existed in one form or another for more than six centuries. As late as the end of the eighteenth century it had never occurred to anyone that Great Britain might one day become dependent on foreign countries for her foodstuffs; it was deemed axiomatic that as the population increased the home production of food must be increased proportionately. That indeed happened for a long time. In 1811 the population had been 11,770,000, of whom only 5.1 per cent were fed on imported wheat; in 1841, by which time the population had increased to 17,536,000, the corresponding proportion was only 5.2 per cent.

Early regulations for the import and export of corn were complementary, their purpose being to keep prices steady and avoid sudden fluctuations as the result of a good or bad harvest. When home prices fell, imports were virtually excluded by high protective duties, exports were permitted and the home production of corn was stimulated by the payment of 'bounties' to the growers. When home prices rose there were no more bounties, exports were forbidden and imports became duty free. From about 1815, however, the Corn Laws were only protective. They were no longer concerned with exports and it was the producer, rather than the consumer, who benefited by them.

The free trade *v.* protection controversy is outside the ambit of this book. It is sufficient to record that the whole of the protec-

ibid.

tionist policy, of which the Corn Laws were part, gradually became more and more discredited. The popular outcry was for cheaper food, no matter where it came from. We first modified the Corn Laws in favour of our colonies; eventually a disastrous harvest in 1845 forced the government to give in.

This was the economic and political climate in which young Alfred Savill had been brought up. He was alive to all these considerations, but we have no means of knowing how his mind worked. Clearly, however, he was optimistic about the prospect of an increasing demand for agricultural land as an investment; that would lead to a growing appreciation by landowners of the value of skilled estate management; and that was his job. He decided, wisely as it turned out, to make agricultural estate management the basis of his professional practice.

The first of his managements was close at hand. Loughton is less than two miles north of Chigwell and the Loughton Hall estate belonged to the Maitlands. He was appointed agent either by Mr William Whitaker Maitland, whom he had advised in 1860 in connection with the proposed extension of the Eastern Counties Railway, or by that gentleman's grandson, the Reverend John Whitaker Maitland, who died in 1909.

The Bishops Hall estate, near Lambourne, lies about three miles north-east of Chigwell and still belongs to the Lockwoods. Savill was appointed by Amelius Mark Lockwood, later to become the first Baron Lambourne, whose father had been one of his early clients. Lord Lambourne was Conservative Member for Epping from 1892 to 1917 and became Lord Lieutenant of Essex in 1919, two years after having been raised to the peerage. He was a president of the Royal Horticultural Society and a personal friend of King Edward VII, whom he entertained at Bishops Hall in 1904. He had no children and the barony became extinct when he died in 1928. The present owner of Bishops Hall is his cousin, Lieutenant-Colonel John Lockwood CBE, barrister-at-law, who was Conservative Member for Hackney 1931-5 and for Romford 1950-5.

There were two Lockwoods in the House of Commons during

the last decade of the nineteenth century. The other, Sir Frank Lockwood, had been Liberal MP for York since 1885 and was Solicitor-General 1894-5. They belonged to opposing parties and there is no evidence that they were related, but both were popular members. Frank Lockwood had a pretty wit and at least one story attributed to him is worth retelling.

The Solicitor-General, accompanied by his wife, was in Edinburgh on official business. It happened that Queen Victoria was there at the same time, and the Lockwoods were bidden to a *levée* at Holyrood House. Naturally they had to go, although Sir Frank, who was not ceremony-minded, would have got out of it had he been able to do so. Possibly Lady Lockwood enjoyed it more than her husband, who found it tedious standing in the seemingly endless queue which moved at a snail's pace through several antechambers towards the throne room. When they came within earshot he learned something which, being a Sassenach, no one had told him. Chiefs of clans, when presented to their Sovereign, are not announced by name but by the names of their ancestral seats. 'Lochiel and Lady Cameron!' . . . 'Auchmaloy and Mrs Buchan' . . . 'Moy and Mrs Mackintosh!' and so forth.

At last they arrived at the head of the queue and a splendidly attired official inclined towards him:

'Your name, Sir, if you please?'

'14 Lennox Gardens and Lady Lockwood.'

But we must come south again to Essex. Loughton, Lambourne and the surrounding district, including Chigwell, have changed greatly in recent years. What in Alfred's time were country villages are now suburbs of London. Inevitably parts of both the Loughton Hall and the Bishops Hall estates have been sold for development and are now built over; the firm of Savills continues to manage what is left of the second.

The Parndon Hall and Mark Hall estates were further afield. Alfred was probably appointed by the Reverend Joseph Arkwright of Mark Hall, who died in 1864; or possibly by that gentleman's son, Loftus Arkwright, of Parndon Hall. Joseph's grandfather was Sir Richard Arkwright who was born in Preston in 1732, began life as a barber, but gave up hairdressing in favour of engineering in the cotton industry. His invention, known as the 'Spinning Jenny', is world-famous. The Parndon Hall and Mark Hall estates ran to more than 5000 acres. Most of the land, including Mark Hall which was demolished, was acquired in the 1950s for the building of Harlow New Town.

But Alfred Savill was not content with practising locally. We have seen that in 1855, when still only 26, he opened an office at 27 Rood Lane in the City of London. In 1870 he moved to 3 St Helen's Place, which belonged to the Worshipful Company of Leathersellers. It is interesting, but fortuitous, that in later years his son, Edwin, was entrusted with the management of the Leathersellers' estates. As there is no record of Alfred's tenancy in the company's books he was probably a subtenant. Eventually, in 1886, he moved to larger premises at 39 New Broad Street, where he practised until his death.

As the outcome of contacts in the City, Savill was entrusted with the management of estates far removed from his native Essex. They included those of the Corys and the Lysaghts, both in South Wales; the Watts House estate at Bishop's Lydeard near Taunton (Boles); the Rousden estate at Lyme Regis (Peek); Dartington Hall (Champernowne) and Fallapit (Ashcombe), both in South Devon; the Dunster and Minehead estates in Somerset (Luttrell). It is said that at one time there were inns and public houses distributed between Anglesey and Plymouth each with a framed photograph of Mr Alfred Savill in the saloon bar.

What in this connection does estate management involve? The answer is a variety of technical operations which in recent years have become more and more complicated. Estate management today, be it urban or rural, consists of much more than the collection of rents, the supervision of repairs and seeing that land is properly farmed. The landowner needs to be advised on many relevant matters that may vitally affect his interests. They include town and country planning, estate development, sales and purchases, the granting and renewal of tenancies, rating, leasehold enfranchisement, and claims for compensation for land compulsorily acquired. Then there is the matter of taxation. Today professional advice to a landowner is influenced, almost before anything, by the impact of current (and possibly future) legislation to do with tax. We have been suffering, and are still suffering, from an apparently ceaseless flood of Acts of Parliament, many of which are ill-digested and obscure. Their repercussions on the ownership of land, the use of land and the value of land are impossible to forecast. One of the depressing consequences is that so much of a land agent's time (the same applies to the lawyer and the accountant) is spent in advising on methods of tax avoidance, rather than on that combination of vision and enterprise which alone spells progress. And King Solomon warned us: 'Where there is no vision the people perish.'

At one time the day-to-day management of an agricultural estate was usually undertaken by a resident land agent or steward – in Scotland called a factor. These men had no technical qualifications and, as we saw earlier, many of the non-resident stewards were attorneys. A resident agent, on the other hand, was frequently a younger son of the owner who had a bent in that direction. Today the resident agent is less common. A landowner is likely to be better served by a member of a firm of surveyors and land agents comprising a number of specialist partners, any one of whom can be consulted at short notice. Where could one expect to find a single person competent to advise on surmounting all, or even most, of the hurdles to be encountered in the wide field of estate management that we have enumerated? He does not exist.

So again with valuation. A whole-time agent, resident on the estate he manages, is unlikely to be a good valuer. The skill of a valuer depends on his ability to assess objectively the many and diverse factors that influence the market from day to day. For that purpose he needs to be *in* the market, buying and selling properties on behalf of clients; that is a matter we shall return to presently.

The appointment of Alfred Savill as a non-resident agent by landowners in so many different parts of the country was a sign of the times. Having started mainly as a builder, he had developed into a surveyor and valuer of keen perception. There was nothing parochial about Savill; he had an ability to interpret portents and events which comes only from the maintenance of wide professional contacts.

So much for the business side of estate management; but the business side is not enough. A good agent, who is tactful and understanding, will gain the good will of the tenants and their co-operation with him as his client's representative. Should he not succeed in doing so, there is a danger that the landlord and his tenants may fail to see each other's points of view and pull in opposite directions. Besides impairing human relationships, that may in the long run depreciate the value of the estate it is his responsibility to enhance.

In a later chapter* we shall discuss agricultural land as an investment. Traditionally it was the policy of the country landowner to let his estate to tenant farmers, except perhaps the home farm. We shall note, however, the increasing security of tenure afforded in recent years to sitting tenants coupled with restrictions on the raising of farm rents. We live today in an inflationary world, and land that can be offered for sale with the benefit of vacant possession is a 'hedge'. There is accordingly a strong incentive to an investor in agricultural land to keep as much of it in hand as possible.

But land so kept has to be farmed, and the day has long passed when the average landowner can afford to farm at a loss. His need to make a profit leads us to describe a development of the traditional business of land agency that has become popular since the end of the Second World War.

'Farm management' is a much more intensive service by a land agent to a landowner than what is understood by 'estate management'. The agent, or a trained farm manager on his staff, takes

*Pages 161–4.

responsibility for nearly everything. In consultation with the client he plans the farming year. Thereafter, subject to an occasional reference back, he is responsible for cropping and tillages, the employment and supervision of labour, marketing, keeping the farm accounts, and for performing all the functions and meeting all the obligations that are consonant with good husbandry. In short, he does the job of the full-time, old fashioned bailiff, but he has wider vision and a higher degree of financial expertise.

The arrangement can be very beneficial to the non-farming landowner. His estate is well farmed and he is relieved of trouble and anxiety. Legally he is still in occupation of the land; he can walk over it, ride over it, shoot over it. Should he have to sell the estate, it is at once available with vacant possession. The economics are carefully worked out. The aim is to make a reasonable annual profit for the owner after allowing the land agent a fair remuneration for the efforts of his farm management department.

If we have conveyed the impression that these services undertaken by a land agent are an entirely new departure, it is false. We have recorded that Alfred Savill (Gen. VII 1829–1905), primarily a builder, farmed between 400 and 500 acres in Chigwell and employed for that purpose a considerable labour force. He was still a young man and there is no evidence of his having owned a farm of that size. A likely explanation is that it was a period of agricultural depression when farm tenants were hard to find, and Mr Savill, land agent, obliged his clients. In 1977 the firm of Savills, through the farm management departments of its country offices, is farming in the region of 200,000 acres.

To revert, however, to estate management as opposed to farm management. The effect of some of the legislation we shall discuss presently is likely, in the long if not in the short run, to be the breaking up of still more of our great agricultural estates. That would be a disaster for more than agriculture. It would be a social tragedy in that it would bring to an end, before many years have passed, that friendly landlord–tenant relationship which has obtained through the centuries and, at its best, has been responsible for so much of what is good in English country life.

We have in mind the kind of estate whose management a land agent – be he whole-time or part-time, resident or non-resident – is likely to enjoy most, and we have explained why today a landowner may think it inadvisable to employ a whole-time resident land agent. But to the agent, if that sort of job comes his way and he prefers a quiet country life to the ever-increasing hurry and scurry of the modern business world, it is undoubtedly attractive. A modest salary (with an adequate pension) is only part of his emoluments. There is a prospect, moreover, of his becoming a close friend of the employer and his employer's family with ample opportunity to learn their likes and dislikes and allow for their foibles. We merely postulate that the candidate for such an agency should make careful inquiry about what will be expected of him if he is appointed. Will the employer concern himself with minor matters or allow his agent a reasonably free hand? If the estate office staff are paid by the owner, what are their duties and who engages them? What professional help from outside specialists will the resident agent be able to rely on? Above all, what are the prospects of continuing ownership; should the employer die, what will happen to the estate – and the agent?

A part-time agent, especially if he has a firm of surveyors behind him, is more independent; but he needs to be adaptable and something of a psychologist. All the estates he looks after are different, each with its own set of problems. A more important consideration is that all the owners are different – in temperament, in their attitudes, in their preferences and prejudices, not least in the demands they make on their agent's time. In his journeying from one estate to the next the agent has constantly to adapt himself to the vagaries of the next client.

At one extreme is the absentee landlord, whom the agent rarely meets and few of whose tenants even know by sight. His agent, answerable to trustees or solicitors, gains the impression that the client is really only interested in the rent roll regardless of nearly everything else. At the other, and pleasanter to work for, is the owner to whom his rents, though important, are not the first consideration. He and his wife live on the property, know all the tenants personally, the names and ages of their children and how they are doing at school, and never forget to inquire after old Tom's back and Martha's headaches. It is comforting to reflect, contrary to the belief of some people who are wilfully ignorant, how many of the great landed estates in this country are still owned by men and women like them.

Between these two extremes are all sorts and conditions of landowners. There is the sporting owner, who has no other interest and whose only confidant is the gamekeeper. There is the time-wasting owner who occupies his agent for the greater part of a busy morning debating the merits and demerits of the new lawn mower. There is the meticulous owner who insists on having explained to him exactly how the claim for compensation has been worked out. And the irresponsible owner who is content to leave the claim to his agent, hopes to get as much as possible, but unhappily has lost the notice to treat.

Undoubtedly the most difficult decision by a non-resident agent, between one client and another, is how much responsibility (or how little) he should take. The late Captain Edward Spencer-Churchill said to Jim Eve,* as he drove him from Northwick Park to the railway station: 'What I like about you, Eve, is that you always allow me to feel *that I still own the estate.*'

To complete the picture, how can an agent secure the good will and co-operation of the tenants? By friendliness of course; by being interested in their affairs; by making time for an occasional chat; by listening patiently to their complaints and giving due consideration to their requests. They all 'count with him', and when he has to refuse a request he gives his reasons and tries to make the tenant feel he has been dealt with fairly. An agent should never voice his thoughts; soliloquies are dangerous. A casual remark such as, 'How much nicer this house would be if

*See page 109.

turned round with the front door at the back' is asking for trouble. Within a fortnight he will receive a letter: 'Dear Sir, I think you should know the builders haven't started yet. . . .'

But Mr Savill would never have made such a foolish remark, and it is time we returned to him.

3

New railways and an old forest

*Alfred Savill and the new railways – the Rocket –
landowners and how they were compensated – Royal
Forest of Waltham (Epping Forest), its history, enclosures
and dedication – Alfred and the manorial lords – 'Alfred
Savill and Sons' – Chigwell Hall – Alfred's death
(1905) – personal note*

We have mentioned that as a valuer, and later an arbitrator,
Savill was closely concerned with claims for compensation for
land compulsorily acquired for the construction of the new railways. And we have seen that there were three railway booms in
his lifetime, the third in the 1860s when he was in his prime and
firmly established in practice.

Early railway experiments, during the first three decades of the
century, had been one consequence of the shortage and high cost
of horse fodder brought about by the Napoleonic Wars; the
possibilities of steam traction were worth investigating. In 1829
George Stephenson had built his famous locomotive, the *Rocket*,
and the first passenger line of any importance was opened the
following year. That was the Liverpool and Manchester Railway
which passed over or under sixty-three bridges, crossed the great
expanse of peat bog called Chat Moss, went through a cutting
two miles long and up to 100 feet deep, and tunnelled under
Liverpool for 2240 yards. The *Rocket* ran daily, thirty-five miles
there and back, at an average speed of sixteen miles per hour and
a maximum of twenty-nine. Besides being a remarkable piece of
engineering the project was a financial success; the railway
carried 71951 passengers between its inauguration on 15 September 1830 and the end of the year.

The Grand Junction Railway was opened in 1837, linking the Liverpool–Manchester line with Birmingham. Then the Great Western Railway, whose engineer was the celebrated Brunel. The South-Eastern Railway came next, closely followed by the London and Brighton Railway, which in 1845 was extended to Chichester. The Great Western Railway was also extended by a line formerly called the London and Bristol. Finally, in 1862, the Great Eastern Railway, with its London terminus in Shoreditch, opened up the whole of East Anglia. In 1845, 2800 miles of railway had been authorized; by 1846, 4540 miles; by 1850, 6580 miles were in operation and upward of 100,000 acres had been acquired from landowners.

Early statutes for the purchase of land for the new railways had been on much the same lines as for turnpikes and canals. But the proposed construction of a railway encountered much fiercer opposition. No country landowner wanted a railway across his estate and many of them took active steps, amounting in some cases to physical warfare, to prevent its happening. The promoters, among whom were not a few irresponsible speculators, found themselves in difficulties. The construction of a railway had to be authorized by a private Act of Parliament; the relevant Bill had to be in the Bills Office by 30 November if there was to be any hope of legislation in the ensuing session, and the Bill had to be accompanied by maps and plans. But the promoters' surveyors had no right to enter upon privately owned land for this purpose, and in any case it was impossible to begin their surveys until the crops had been harvested. Because of the short time available there was an immense demand for land surveyors, some of whom, employed at grossly exorbitant wages, were so young as to be almost totally inexperienced. It is not surprising that in Parliament their plans were found to be full of inaccuracies; another reason for their inaccuracy being that so much of the land had been surveyed surreptitiously after dark with the aid of bull's-eye lanterns.

The provisions of the first of the private Acts for the construction of railways varied considerably. As regards compensation, however, they all followed the precedent of the earlier Acts for turnpikes and canals, which had required disputes about compensation to be determined by a jury. The Lands Clauses Consolidation Act of 1845 sought to achieve some measure of uniformity. It made rules and regulations for procedure and prescribed a series of model clauses for inclusion by citation in subsequent Acts. A dissatisfied claimant might still elect for a jury, but another method, under the provisions of the 1845 Act, was to refer the issue to one or more arbitrators. If the claimant and the promoters were able to agree on the appointment of a single arbitrator, his decision on the facts was final. An alternative method was for each party to appoint his own arbitrator, in which event, before hearing evidence, the two arbitrators appointed an umpire to decide between them if that should become necessary.

The basis of compensation was not merely market value, but market value plus a supplement to compensate the owner for the fact that his land was being taken compulsorily. The supplement could be as high as 25 per cent, or even 50 per cent. In their evidence before a Select Committee of the House of Lords on lands taken by railways (1845), Mr John Clutton and Mr Edward Driver, two distinguished surveyors of the day, gave as their opinion that the percentage supplement should be 'very high'. Alfred Savill will have subscribed to that view and there is little doubt that his decisions, when sitting as an arbitrator, reflected it.

Another department of Savill's professional activities which is interesting, and perhaps in retrospect one of the most valuable, was in connection with the enclosures of Epping Forest. The history of our great forests has been described as an important part of the history of England, and the part he played requires a brief historical introduction.

Epping Forest is what survives of the great forest of Essex, which once covered the greater part of the county. From the Norman Conquest until the Commonwealth it was known as the

Royal Forest of Waltham, taking its name from the rich Augustinian abbey in the ancient town of Waltham on its western border. The only other town in the region was Barking at the southern end of the county; here a nunnery under royal patronage had developed from a Saxon foundation. These two religious houses owned most of the land in the forest, but their ownership was subject to the right of the Crown to hunt over it and control any development that might interfere with the exercise of that right. The game, besides a great variety of wild fowl, included the wolf, the wild boar, the badger and the red and fallow deer. 'In the forests are the kings' places of retirement and their chief delights; for to them they come for hunting when they lay aside their cares.'

On a perambulation in 1641 it was found that Waltham Forest extended to nearly 60000 acres. Apart from the two towns, it consisted of mile after mile of uncultivated waste and woodland, interspersed here and there with small clearings. In some of these were primitive settlements whose inhabitants were mostly forest workers and squatters, who had been granted rights to pasture their cattle and lop timber in compensation for having to submit to the harsh restrictions of the forest laws. When the monasteries were dissolved by Henry VIII the land became vested in the Crown, and much of it was granted to court favourites who enlarged the clearings and began a process of enclosure; much of this was undertaken without authority and in a manner later held to be illegal.

The enforcement of the forest laws, some of which dated from Edward the Confessor, was entrusted to several categories of officers of the Crown. At their head was the steward, later known as the Lord Warden; this hereditary office was held for three hundred years by the proud de Veres, Earls of Oxford. The local judicial officers were the 'verderers' who presided over the 'courts of attachment', which heard and determined applications to enclose besides dealing with unlawful enclosures and minor offences. By and large, the administration of the forest on behalf of the Crown after the Dissolution is not a very creditable story.

It became more and more lax. The royal favourites who had settled in the district had great power and rode rough-shod over the commoners, carving out bits of the forest to enlarge their demesnes: 'Here a cantle, and there a snippet, here a slab and there a slice . . . a bare piece of turf or a wooded clump.' Perhaps it is understandable that the verderers lost heart and in the early nineteenth century, when unlawful enclosures reached scandalous proportions, came to the conclusion that there was really nothing they could do about it. They even came to doubt whether their ancient powers still existed and were reluctant to impose penalties which they might be unable to enforce.

But it was not only the well-to-do landowners who had come to treat the forest laws with contempt. They were frequently broken by the commoners themselves. Thus on Goldings, Baldwins and York Hills, near Loughton, were hundreds of squatters who had built shacks and hovels, enclosing bits of the forest for that purpose. Some of the local landowners approved of those squatter enclosures on the ground that the poor had to live somewhere, and that the ownership of even a small piece of land created a sense of responsibility. One of the verderers for this part of Essex was Mr William Whitaker Maitland of Loughton Hall, whom we have mentioned already. He went as far as to buy up these smallholdings when they became available, build cottages on them, fence them, and either let or resell them. When he died in 1861 his grandson, the Reverend John Whitaker Maitland, who succeeded him as lord of the manor of Loughton, continued this practice.

There had been protests in the 1840s at failure by the verderers to enforce the forest laws; no court of attachment had been convened for nearly twenty years. At a public meeting in the summer of 1843 they were accused of neglecting their duties and a petition was prepared demanding some positive action. At long last, in 1849, a parliamentary commission was appointed. Its terms of reference were to examine rights and claims over Waltham Forest (also the New Forest), ascertain boundaries, investigate encroachments and unlawful enclosures, and review the nature and jurisdiction of the forest courts. Parliament was not helpful to the commoners. One outcome of the commission's report was the disafforestation, in 1851, of Hainault Forest, a part of Waltham Forest east of the River Roding, on the ground that the Crown was being put to considerable expense in maintaining its rights for the benefit of local inhabitants without any advantage either to the Crown or the public.

The enclosures persisted and forestal rights belonging to the Crown continued to be sold off. The inevitable clash came in 1865, when Thomas Willingale, head of a family of commoners who had exercised their right of lopping for many years and were determined to retain it, agreed to lead a revolt against the enclosing landowners. He was supported financially by an outstanding Radical of that period, Sir Thomas Fowell Buxton, and by other neighbours. The revolt led to Willingale's appearance before the Epping magistrates on a charge of injuring forest trees. The chairman of the bench was the Reverend John Whitaker Maitland of Loughton Hall who, as we have seen, had followed the example of his grandfather; together they had enclosed many hundreds of acres in the Goldings district, asserting that they had a right to do so. Even at that time the legality of the Maitland enclosures was questionable, but it is to the credit of the reverend gentleman, who was Willingale's arch-enemy, that the charge was dismissed. The following year, however, Samuel Willingale, a nephew of Thomas, was among a number of commoners charged at Waltham Abbey with a similar offence. On this occasion they were all convicted. According to a contemporary report, they 'behaved with considerable levity in court' and elected to serve seven days' imprisonment with hard labour rather than pay the fines imposed.

This was only the beginning of a long series of wrangles between the commoners and the lord of the manor of Loughton and other manorial lords in that part of the county. In 1854 the Corporation of the City of London had come into the picture as a result of their purchasing 200 acres of forest land for use as a cemetery. The Corporation had thus acquired commoner status, and from then onward the lords were confronted by potentially powerful adversaries. In 1863 the House of Commons petitioned the Crown against any further sales of Crown lands to facilitate enclosures, and later in the same year a select committee was appointed to consider, among other things, what steps should be taken to conserve the remaining open spaces. The committee reported that more than 7000 acres were still unenclosed and recommended that no further enclosures should be allowed.

The matter was allowed to drag on, and any parliamentary action that might have ensued was stayed pending a decision by the Court of Chancery in a suit brought by the City Corporation. Incensed by what they deemed an illegal enclosure of land adjoining their cemetery, the Corporation had brought an action against all the manorial lords who had recently enclosed lands. The case did not come on for hearing until 1864, and the decision went in favour of the Corporation. The Master of the Rolls severely censured persons who had taken what did not belong to them, without authority, and had 'endeavoured to support their title by a large amount of false evidence'.

The next step by the Corporation was to acquire the soil of the forest. An Act passed in 1871 had enabled them to acquire and maintain open spaces near London, but outside the metropolis, for the recreation of Londoners. They had been afforded borrowing powers for that purpose. The Corporation now decided to apply all their available resources to rescuing what was left of the Essex wastes; within a few years they had purchased 5600 acres together with any Crown rights attaching.

Eventually came the Essex Forest Act of 1878 in final settlement. Enclosures made before 14 August 1851 were allowed to stand; also enclosures made subsequently of land which had been built on at that date or occupied as private gardens. The whole of the forest lands were disafforested in law. The Queen was empowered to appoint a Ranger and appointed her son, the Duke of Connaught. The Corporation of the City of London became Conservators of the Forest with a duty to keep it unbuilt on and to protect and manage it as a public open space. Lands that had been illegally enclosed since 1851 were thrown open, and the owners of lands not thrown open were to be made to pay for their titles. The amounts, together with amounts of compensation payable to persons dispossessed, were to be fixed by an arbitrator whose awards were binding.

It is only natural that Alfred Savill should have been professionally concerned in all these matters affecting Epping Forest. He was an acknowledged authority on copyholds and the manorial tenure of land and had practised in the county all his life. In the early 1870s he was already retained as professional adviser to a number of Essex lordships; they included the manors of Chigwell, West Hatch, Waltham Holy Cross, Woolston, Housham, Fyfield, Paslow and Benfleet.

The arbitrator appointed under the 1878 Act was Sir Arthur (later Lord) Hobhouse. The lords of the manors throughout the forest combined to employ Alfred Savill to represent them as their surveyor and valuer. The arbitrations continued for four years, during which Hobhouse conducted 114 public inquiries, many private inquiries, and made 787 orders. Eventually he issued his final award, to which was annexed a map of the area which thereafter was to constitute Epping Forest.

It remains to add that on 6 May 1882, at High Beech, Queen Victoria declared Epping Forest open to the public. 'And thus,' wrote W. R. Fisher, 'by the exertions and at the sole cost of the Corporation of London, a district taken from the ancient folkland for the exclusive use of the sovereigns, was, after many centuries, dedicated by the hands of their successor to the use and enjoyment of her subjects.'*

So much for Alfred Savill the man of business – first a builder's clerk, then a builder in a village near London, later a part-time valuer and estate agent practising locally, eventually a land agent and surveyor with a national reputation. He was a friend and

* *The Forest of Essex*, 1887.

contemporary of John Clutton and Edward Ryde who were co-fathers of the Institution of Surveyors in 1868, and of Julian Rogers who was its first secretary. The foundation of the Institution was largely due to the influence of the Land Surveyors' Club, which dates from 1834. Alfred Savill was not elected to that club until later, but in 1868 he became a founder member of the Institution under the presidency of John Clutton; in 1868 there were 131 corporate members. The name was changed shortly to the Surveyors' Institution, and in 1880 it was granted a royal charter by Queen Victoria. In 1930 the name was changed again to the Chartered Surveyors' Institution. Eventually, in 1946, it became the Royal Institution of Chartered Surveyors, and at the time of writing its corporate membership exceeds 36000.

John Clutton, who was the most eminent surveyor at that date, has been described as a 'forthright professional man of undoubted integrity'; no reference to his presidency, however brief, would be complete without the citation of a passage in his Opening Address. He regretted a tendency by surveyors and valuers to abrogate their true function, which was to be objective, and become partisan: 'The business of a surveyor, I hold to be, is to give an unbiased opinion on the subject placed before him, and not to become in any way an advocate.' By way of illustration he told a story which, it may be thought, points a moral for not a few surveyors and valuers today. A respected surveyor, one of John Clutton's contemporaries, was about to enter the witness box when the arbitrator inquired of him: 'I think you are concerned for Lord So-and-So?' He answered: 'Sir, I am *employed* by Lord So-and-So; I am not *concerned* for him.'

Alfred Savill's wife, *née* Eleanor Hallings Smith, died in 1893. The eldest son was Alfred (Gen. VIII, 1854–1928). His father took him into partnership in 1886 and moved the office from St Helen's Place to 39 New Broad Street; thereafter the firm was renamed Alfred Savill and Son. This second Alfred was essentially a countryman and concentrated on the management of its agricultural estates. He became a verderer of Epping Forest in 1908 and retired from practice in the early 1920s. The second son,

Arthur Edward (1862–1943), lived in Chigwell all his life and was a partner in the City firm of solicitors, Druces and Attlee. The third and fifth sons, Edwin (1868–1947) and Henry Norman (1874–1945), became partners in Alfred Savill and Sons in 1902 and 1905 respectively. The fourth son, Robert Cecil (1871–1952), was a delicate child and never allowed to go into business.

Alfred Savill, his widowed mother, his wife and children and several grandchildren were not the only Savills who lived in Chigwell during the second half of the nineteenth century. Alfred's uncle, Joseph Savill (Gen. VI, 1798–1876), a farmer, lived at a house called Ten Mile Villa. Two of his aunts lived in Chigwell. So did two of his brothers and their families – Philip, the brewer, and Martin Savill; also two of his sisters, one of whom married George Gould.

These nineteenth-century Savills had something in common with the Forsytes, though a claim that *The Forsyte Saga* was based on the Savills has no evidence to support it. Any untoward happening at the instance of, or affecting, a Savill became the subject of a family inquest. It was conducted by the members individually as well as in concert, and there was much tut-tutting, raising of eyebrows and shaking of heads behind their respective front doors. The verdict was seldom unanimous, and by the time that stage was reached the happening had assumed an importance that was totally unrealistic. Eleanor Savill's carriage accident was an example.

The facts on the face of them were simple enough. The horse had bolted and the carriage overturned. Eleanor was thrown out. She was badly bruised and shocked, but not seriously injured.

The event caused a great stir in Chigwell among the Savills, the Smiths and their more distant relations. An inquest was opened. 'When did it happen? Why did it happen? Whose fault was it? Was it likely to happen again?' It was a talking point, and eventually became a kind of chronological milestone for the dating of other events:

'Was that *before*, or *after*, Eleanor was run away with by the horse?'

This was later shortened to 'the horse' and passed into Savill terminology as indicating a long time ago:

'My dear, how *are* you? I haven't seen you since the horse!'

There were a number of societies, guilds and committees in Chigwell, on most of which the Savill family were represented. They were also represented on the local authority. One of the Savills, a councillor, decided to leave the district and resigned. When his resignation was announced a fellow councillor heaved a sigh of relief. 'Thank God!' he exclaimed. 'At last Chigwell is beginning to become *unsavillized.*'

In the early 1870s Alfred Savill decided to build himself a new house in Chigwell. He chose a site on rising ground to the north-west of the road from Woodford Bridge to Chelmsford (now the A113); it is next to Chigwell church and has a superb view to the south. Chigwell grammar school is a few hundred yards north-east of it and The King's Head, where Charles Dickens lodged, is on the opposite side of the road.

He appointed as his architect Richard Norman Shaw, and had a special reason for doing so. Norman Shaw was a younger brother of that brilliant young man, Robert Ewart Shaw, who in the 1850s together with young Walter Savill threw up his job with Willis, Cann and Company, started in business as a shipbroker, and jointly with Walter Savill founded the Shaw Savill and Albion Line. Norman Shaw, born and educated in Edinburgh, had later moved to London and in the 1870s was firmly established as one of the leading architects in the country. His best known city building is New Scotland Yard on the Thames Embankment, but in 1871 he had built a new head office for Shaw Savill in Leadenhall Street. Shaw is better known for his houses and he specialized in building for artists. Chigwell Hall, completed in 1876, is the only country house he is believed to have built in Essex. Its red-brick walls, gabled tiled roof and white sash-barred windows are typical of his work. And it is typical of his period that the house had between fifteen and twenty bedrooms but only one bathroom, and that on the second floor. The Hall and its extensive grounds now belong to the Metropolitan Police and are used by them as a country club.

Savill was neighbourly and open-handed; he took an active interest in local affairs, especially in later life when he had the time available. He was a member of the Essex County Council, and for thirty-eight years a governor of Chigwell grammar school where he himself had been educated. He enlarged at his own expense the ancient parish church ('Rather a pity I think', wrote one of his grandchildren!) and became a churchwarden. He died at Chigwell Hall on 24 March 1905 in his 77th year.

Apart from his business and public activities, what sort of person was he? One gains the impression of a very intelligent, hard-working man who knew his own mind and was not afraid to speak it. No doubt Alfred inherited these and other qualities from his parents and especially from his mother, including her sense of humour. He enjoyed good living and was a generous host; when he died, the cellars at Chigwell Hall were found to be stocked with superb port – the '63, '70, '73, '96 and 1900. He could, however, be formidable, and Colonel John Lockwood of Lambourne, who remembers him well, has described Mr Savill as 'the prototype of John Bull'. His portrait bears that out. Kindly man that he was, there is evidence that on occasion the younger members of the family stood in awe of him. His grandson, Eric Savill,* recalls one of those occasions when the boy was 8. The story is best told in Eric's words:

I once stayed at Chigwell Hall when I got into hot water. There was a pond in the grounds with some exotic duck to grace it. My first night I put down a night line with twelve hooks for eels. Rising early next morning, in eager anticipation, I found the pond was complete chaos; twelve of my grandfather's cherished ducks were well and truly hooked in their crops. I was not asked to stay again. . . .

His grandfather lived in four reigns, including the whole of the reign of Queen Victoria, and into the first decade of the new

*Now Sir Eric Savill: see page 75.

century. He was a true Victorian. His life and behaviour reflected the outstanding characteristics of the English upper middle class during that relatively stable period: high principles, a keen sense of responsibility, unshakable confidence in its own destiny, a satisfactory consciousness of moral rectitude. The Queen's death had marked the end of an epoch. And Alfred Savill, in the splendid phrasing of the early Quakers, 'having finished his day's work in his day, joined his ancient brethren who were gone before'.

4

Edwin Savill *v.* Lloyd George

*Three Savill brothers: Alfred (Gen. VIII, 1854–1928),
Edwin (1868–1947), Norman (1874–1945) – state of
the countryside – and of the towns – David Lloyd George
and his 'People's Budget' – Edwin Savill and the Land
Union – the 'single-taxer' – The Land Report and The
Land Retort*

For ten years before Alfred Savill died the country had had a
Conservative ('Unionist') government, first under the premiership
of A. J. Balfour and latterly the Marquess of Salisbury. At a
general election in December 1905, less than a year after Alfred's
death; the Liberals were returned to power. Sir Henry Campbell-
Bannerman became Prime Minister (to be succeeded by Asquith
in 1908) and David Lloyd George became, first, President of the
Board of Trade, and later, in 1908, Chancellor of the Exchequer.
As Chancellor, Lloyd George at last saw the opportunity to put
into practice some of the theories he had cherished ever since he
entered Parliament in 1890. One of his principal objectives was
'land reform'. Landowners were confronted by radical proposals,
not the least drastic of which was the taxation of what was described as 'unearned increment' in land value. That is to say, an
increase in the value of the soil which is not attributable to any
exertion on the part of the landowner and therefore, according
to the theories of John Stuart Mill and other economists, should
rightfully belong to the State. Mill's American contemporary,
Henry George, went further; he wanted to see all existing land
values taxed, no matter whence they derived. Edwin Savill
(Gen. VIII, 1868–1947) was to become deeply involved in fighting
the Lloyd George proposals; before, however, we embark on that

story it may be helpful to examine some of the factors that were affecting land ownership and land use at the time.

When Jonathan Savill (Gen. VII), Edwin's grandfather, died in 1849, the country was on the road to a complete recovery from the first great agricultural depression of the nineteenth century. The industrial revolution was well under way and the rapid growth of the industrial population was creating an unprecedented demand for agricultural produce. The rents of farms had been adjusted to the new conditions, and since the coming into force of the Tithe Commutation Act of 1836 the incidence of tithe had ceased to be a bar to enterprise and experiment. The railways were beginning to provide efficient, long-distance transport. The future was promising, and young Alfred may be thought to have begun to build up his practice as a land agent at just the right moment.

For ten or more years there was steady progress, subject to minor recessions reflecting commercial setbacks which always tend to affect the prosperity of agriculture. But in the early 1860s (As Lord Ernle put it*) the tide ceased to flow and after about 1874 it ebbed rapidly. It was the beginning of the second great agricultural depression of the nineteenth century, which was to last until after the end of the reign of Queen Victoria.

1870 had seen the outbreak of the Franco-Prussian War. Great Britain was not involved, but every European war has had a profound effect, if only temporary, on certain of our industries. At one extreme the manufacturers of luxury goods, dependent on foreign markets which no longer exist, can be forced out of business. At the other, the manufacturers of armaments and of equipment and clothing for the armed forces, whether the armed forces become involved or not, are sure to benefit even after taxation of their excess profits. An army, moreover, not only has to be fed; it needs to be well fed. We have it on good authority that 'Napoelon's armies always used to march on their stomachs

*English Farming, Past and Present, 6th edition, 1961.

shouting *"Vive l'Interieur"*.'* The well-being of '*l'Interieur*' is primarily the responsibility of the farmer, and as long as other nations continue fighting one another, or us, he has little to fear from foreign competition in the shape of imported foodstuffs. Prices rise, wages rise, farms are only to be had at a premium.

When the war ends there comes a reckoning. We saw earlier how the first great agricultural depression of the century resulted from the catastrophic fall in prices that followed the Napoleonic Wars. The Franco-Prussian War and its aftermath were a repeat performance. Both France and Germany ceased to be competitors; prices soared and so did profits; there was reckless bidding by farmers for more land.

Peace was signed in May of the following year and, as before, the rot set in quickly. Foreign competition began again; all too soon the demands upon our major industries had returned to normal. Agriculture was one, and several bad seasons in succession made things worse. Farms became untenanted and, because their cultivation was no longer profitable, great areas of corn land were put down to grass. Between 1871 and 1901 the corn lands in England and Wale sshrank from 8,244,393 acres to 5,886,052 acres; and the depression reached its bottom in 1894-5, when the price of wheat per imperial quarter fell to less than 23 shillings – the lowest for 150 years.

Alas for farmers, the old maxim, 'Down corn, up horn; down horn, up corn', no longer applied. Until about 1877 imports of live sheep and cattle had been mainly from European countries; from then onward America and Canada joined in competition and our imports of dead meat rapidly increased. New Zealand and Argentina followed suit and it is on record that imported mutton, which in 1882 did not exceed 181,000 cwt, most of it boiled or tinned, had risen by 1899 to $3\frac{1}{2}$ million cwt of frozen carcases. It is not surprising that great numbers of skilled and able-bodied men, who had laboured on the land all their lives,

*W. L. Sellar and R. J. Yeatman, *1066 And All That*, 1930.

found themselves out of work and with no prospect of getting any.

A further consequence of the depression was that the owners of agricultural estates, who had been the principal providers of houses in country districts for occupation by their work people, gave up building; many landowners were no longer able to afford to keep their existing houses in repair. Thus a housing problem was created as well as an employment problem. The great industrial towns had long been acting as a magnet to the rural population, who hoped to better themselves; the depression strengthened that inducement, and from the early 1870s there was a continuing exodus from the countryside into the rapidly developing urban areas.

Not that the urban developments (no doubt there were exceptions) had anything to commend them. Cheap houses were needed to accommodate the influx of recruits to the newly established industries. There were no restrictions, no bylaws, no prescribed standards and town planning had not been heard of; the heyday of the worst type of speculative builder had arrived. Two tiers of profit were looked for. The first by the builder, who sold his houses to the investor at the highest prices obtainable; the second by the investor, who let them to the workers at the highest rents he could get. To swell the profits building costs were cut to a minimum and as many houses as possible, most of them without indoor sanitation or even a water supply, were crowded on to the land – often cheek by jowl with tall warehouses, congested workshops, and William Blake's 'satanic mills'. Wages were low and the rents were more than many of the disillusioned tenants could afford. So two or more families would double up and share accommodation that had been designed for only one. In the result, thousands of the new houses became slums on the day they were first occupied.

The first legislation of significance to prevent the creation of further slums was the Public Health Act of 1875, which empowered local authorities to make bylaws and regulations. But compliance with the regulations increased building costs and put the

new houses even further out of reach of the people who needed
them most. The existing slums became more overcrowded than
ever. The report of a royal commission in 1885 awakened the
public conscience and paved the way for the Housing of the
Working Classes Act 1890. It enabled local authorities to close
and demolish slum property and build houses to let. But until
1914 no financial assistance was available from the central
government, in consequence of which the Act had no noticeable
effect. The local authorities were ready enough to demolish slums,
but understandably reluctant to replace them at the sole expense
of the ratepayers.

The last ten years of the nineteenth century are sometimes
referred to as the 'gay nineties'. It may be thought that the gaiety
was largely confined to those so fortunate as to have been born
into the right social class. Then came the Boer War, and the
Queen died before the Treaty of Vereeniging which ended it;
our relations with foreign powers were again friendly. By the
time of Alfred Savill's death in 1905 the second great agricultural depression had begun to lift. It was a period of scientific
and industrial advancement, and income tax was one shilling in
the pound.* Yet in spite of this progress poverty was widespread
and our working-class population, by and large, were under and
badly housed.

This was the background against which Lloyd George, in
April 1909, introduced in the House of Commons what came
to be known as the 'People's Budget'. Whatever its faults, it was
the sort of budget one would expect from a man who all through
his life had been the champion of the underdog, hated oppression,
and was bitterly opposed to any entrenchment of privilege. His
budget was his declaration of war on poverty. In it he proposed
new forms of taxation to pay for the great expansion of the social
services in connection with health, housing, employment and
wages, which he had long deemed necessary.

*On incomes between £2000 and £3000 per annum; on incomes over
£3000 per annum it was 1s. 3d.

When Lloyd George's Finance Bill eventually reached the Statute Book, having precipitated a general election in the process, it was said to have occupied more parliamentary time than any other government measure within living memory. Part I, the most controversial, provided for four new taxes (described as 'duties') on land. They were 'increment value duty', 'reversion duty', 'undeveloped land duty' and 'mineral rights duty'.

'Increment value duty' was to be 20 per cent of the difference between 'assessable site value' determined at the appointed day, and the corresponding value determined at the date of sale or death. It thus fell to be levied at irregular and fortuitous intervals.

'Reversion duty' was to be 10 per cent of any increase in the 'total value' (i.e. of land plus buildings) over the corresponding value at the date the lease was granted. Normally, the increase would represent the value of buildings erected during the term of the lease, plus any enhancement of the value of the site; it was to be payable when the lease expired.

'Undeveloped land duty' was to be a halfpenny in the pound per annum* on the assessable site value of land that had not been developed by the erection of houses, or of commercial or industrial buildings other than for purposes of agriculture; and of land not built on and not used for commercial or industrial purposes other than agriculture.

'Mineral rights duty' was to be a shilling in the pound on the rental value of rights to work minerals and on mineral wayleaves.

These proposals met with vehement opposition in Parliament from the Tory benches, and from a great variety of persons and bodies outside. One of the first steps taken by the opponents was the formation of the Land Defence League, later renamed the Land Union. Its first chairman was Mr Newton Robinson, shortly to be replaced by Captain N. G. Pretyman MP. Its vice-

*One halfpenny in the pound may sound innocuous. But this was an *annual* tax on a *capital* value. If the rental value was calculated at 4 per cent, the undeveloped land duty was equivalent to over one shilling in the pound per annum.

chairman for twenty-five years was Edwin Savill. The member-ship included landowners and persons interested in the land, agriculturists, surveyors and land agents, architects, builders, lawyers, bankers, together with a number of county councils and other local authorities. Captain Pretyman was not a man who minced words. At a general meeting of the Land Union he said its purpose was 'to bring home to the country a sense of the injustice and the mischievous character of the land taxes, which have introduced into politics a spirit of dishonesty . . . and a policy of confiscation unknown in any other parliament in this country or elsewhere'.

Having brought that home, the Union was there to defend the interests represented by its members by every means available. In Parliament this was to be done by instructing and briefing members of the Opposition; outside Parliament by educating the public in what the Lloyd George proposals amounted to, warning them of the consequences that would inevitably ensue, and enlisting nation-wide support by public meetings, lectures and literature.

The Surveyors' Institution, though most of its members were strongly opposed to the proposals, wisely confined itself to revealing and underlining some of the fallacies that underlay them and their technical, rather than political, consequences. Later it was suggested in some quarters that the Institution ought to have taken more vigorous action, and the chairman of one of its provincial branches went as far as to say that the Institution should have done the job in defence of landowners that was actually done by Edwin Savill and his fellow members of the Land Union. That criticism was unwarranted. The Union was a highly pow-ered political organization. The surveyor (or any other profes-sional man) is entitled to his political opinions *as an individual* and free as such to express them. A professional society, comprising a body of persons whose opinions differ, must never enter the party-political arena.

In fact, the observations by the council of the Surveyors' Institution, contained in a memorandum submitted to the

Chancellor in May 1909, were practical and to the point. They were also couched in moderate language and are likely to have converted to the cause of the Opposition more people, so far uncommitted, than the vituperations of Captain Pretyman.

In connection with increment value duty, the council objected to the over-frequent use of the tendentious expression 'unearned increment'. They said that more often than not this was a misnomer. It was conceded that there had been cases where 'extraordinary profit' had accrued to landowners as a result of happenings that had suddenly created a demand for their land. But they said this was exceptional, and that in most cases an increase in the value of land was a slow process. If, as often happened, there had been several changes in ownership, the only owner caught for the new tax (the whole of it) would be the last. They contended that the same applied to reversion duty. Leasehold interests, like freehold interests, frequently change hands during the term; the nearer the reversion the higher the premium accruing to the assignor. Why, they asked, should the assessable value be the difference in values between the beginning of the lease and the end of it, and the reversioner be expected to pay tax on the lot? As to undeveloped land duty, the council pointed out that speculative builders tend to buy the land they propose to build on well in advance of their requirements. If that land was to be taxed in the meantime, they would become more cautious; this would hinder the development and have precisely the converse effect of that which the government intended.

Edwin Savill, as vice-chairman of the Land Union, was in the front line of the attackers, notwithstanding that he was a partner in a busy firm. The author of an article written more than thirty years later, describing the fighting spirit of the early members, said: 'The name of Sir Edwin Savill [as he later became] will never be forgotten.' His strength lay largely in the fact that, being himself an experienced valuer, he was able to call in aid a fund of expert knowledge that most of his colleagues lacked. He was in a position, for example, not only to foretell the likely consequences of the Lloyd George proposals, but to point to technical deficiencies of the Bill itself, which, he claimed, would make it unworkable.

It was indeed ridiculous and unnecessarily complicated. The type of measure relating to the land which makes one wonder whether the parliamentary draftsman ever stops to ask himself: 'What sort of a chap is an Inland Revenue valuer? Is he a human being with undoubted gifts, but subject to human limitations? Or is he a god-like creature in whom are collated the judgement of a Solomon, the discernment of an Aristotle, the imagination of a Michelangelo and the foresight of a Major Prophet?'

Part I of the Bill prescribed no less than five different values to be determined in respect of each hereditament. In defining 'gross value' the draftsman employed 61 words; 'full site value' 105 words; 'total value' 173 words; 'assessable site value' 472 words. The fact that 'agricultural value' was so well understood as not to require a new statutory definition must have been a big disappointment.

The Bill passed the Commons and was sent to the Lords. Although the Lords still had power to reject a Money Bill passed by the Lower House, they had not done so for some time. On this occasion, however, they exercised their power and rejected it. Asquith asked the King to dissolve Parliament, and on 10 January 1910 there was a general election. The Liberal government were returned and at once resubmitted the Finance Bill to the Lords. This time the Lords gave it their consent and it was enacted as the Finance (1909–10) Act 1910.*

The valuation, to be undertaken by the Valuation Office of the Inland Revenue, then proceeded. Ten years later it was nearly complete, but a number of appeals and objections were outstanding. By the Finance Act 1920 (section 57) the duties imposed under Part I of the Act of 1910, except for mineral rights duty,

*At another general election in December 1910 the government sought, and obtained, a mandate to abrogate the power of the House of Lords to veto the provisions of Money Bills. When the Prime Minister threatened to advise the creation of enough Liberal peers to swamp the Upper House, the Parliament Act 1911 went through and remains the law.

were repealed by the coalition government which came into power in December 1918. The obligation to complete the valuation was cancelled, and any payments of duty that had been made were refunded. Sir Edgar Harper FSI, who had been Chief Valuer of the Inland Revenue at the material time, wrote in his retirement: 'These complications [i.e. due to errors in Part I] were the cause of the difficulties experienced in the working of the Act and of its ultimate failure.'

Before we leave the subject of Lloyd George's Land Taxes, brief mention must be made of another group, mainly Liberal, who opposed Part I of the 1909–10 Finance Bill for a different reason. They were not connected with the Land Union, which indeed had been formed to fight them, and during the debates in Parliament the two groups were constantly at each other's throats.

The United Committee for the Taxation of Land Values (it has changed its title from time to time) was established in the 1880s and is sometimes described as the 'single-tax movement'. Its members base themselves on the philosophy of the American political economist, Henry George (1839–97), who urged that in the interests of social and economic justice all private ownership of land should be abolished. Their argument runs like this:

Land is the original source of all consumption and capital goods. Every article we use is composed of materials that come from land or have been worked up into the desired form by labour and capital. The use of land is therefore basic and vital to all production. . . . Those who believe in equality of opportunity cannot believe that it is fair that some members of society should be allowed to appropriate truly unearned incomes, many of them quite enormous, from the possession of sites made highly valuable by the presence and activities of the community.

It might be expected, as a corollary to the proposition, that Henry George was in favour of nationalizing the land. On the contrary, he condemned it for political, economic and practical reasons, discussion of which is outside the ambit of this book. But perhaps the most obvious practical difficulty, from his point of view, was that in practice the State – or any other purchaser for that matter – cannot acquire land without at the same time acquiring, and being saddled with the responsibility for managing, buildings and other immovable objects attached to it. It was a main plank of Henry George's platform that *individual* enterprise, *individual* effort and *individual* management should be encouraged.

His proposed remedy for the injustices, which he held to result from private ownership, fell far short of a policy for nationalization. His remedy was the levying of a single universal tax on all land values, whether the land was developed by buildings, undeveloped, or used for agriculture. He had calculated that the amount of such a tax, in aggregate, would be large enough to replace all other rates and taxes and thus relieve industry of an immense burden. We should rid ourselves once and for all of the anomaly that a man is 'fined' by the Exchequer and the local authority in proportion to the wealth he has created by his own efforts. Furthermore, runs the argument, the landowner would have a continual inducement to put his land to the most profitable use, seeing that he would have to pay the same amount in tax whether its use was prudent or not.

The validity of this proposition has been confirmed by distinguished English economists and financial experts. Others, no less distinguished, have denied it. Among the former are not a few experienced surveyors and valuers who are attracted by the idea; they think that some kind of governmental experiment, possibly within a circumscribed area, is overdue. It is untrue to say, as do some who ought to know better, that the 'taxation of land values' was tried under the 1910 Finance Act and failed. In the sense in which that form of taxation is understood by the single-taxer, it has never been tried in this country.

The United Committee welcomed the Lloyd George proposal for a valuation of all land in England and Wales. That at least was a step in the right direction. What they deplored was the use the government intended to make of it. The committee stood, and still stand, for the taxation of 'land value', by which they mean *all* of land value. The proposals were merely for taxing *parts* of the value, provided it was found possible (which it wasn't) to distinguish and separate those parts from other parts. 'Land value tax,' said the United Committee, was a misnomer: a so-called increment in value was no more the 'value' of the land than the lid of a pot is the pot.

It is interesting to note that Edwin Savill, after failure by the Land Union to prevent the Finance Bill reaching the Statute Book himself had thoughts on these lines. He professed to want to maintain the *status quo*; but it is evident, from a paper he read to the Surveyors' Institution in February 1912, that he saw a need for change – at any rate in our system of local taxation. He suggested that the Institution should appoint a 'strong committee' to investigate the principles of the taxation of land values, take evidence from persons with specialized knowledge, and produce an objective report.

This apparent *volte face* by the vice-chairman of a militant body at which, so recently, the United Committee for the Taxation of Land Values had been hurling abuse, must have astonished his hearers. An indignant reader of the *Land Agents' Record* wrote sarcastically that Mr Savill had 'described the schemes of the *committee with a long name* for confiscating the entire value of the bare land in a beautiful spirit of toleration'. The journal of the United Committee, however, made the following comment:

This is a very commendable suggestion, and we hope that the Institution will proceed with a really impartial consideration of the subject.... We agree emphatically that a report such as Mr Savill proposes would give people an opportunity of judging for themselves, and would be much appreciated by large numbers who now have to rely entirely upon literature and speeches showing one side of the case only.

If it was not yet safe for the lion to lie down with the lamb (the reader must judge which was which) at least they had come to occupy the same field. And possibly the vice-chairman of the Land Union was seen not to be such a reactionary Tory as some people had supposed.

But he continued to make war on the Liberals, principally on account of their agricultural policies. A small group, self-styled the 'Land Enquiry Committee', who described themselves as 'friends of the present government', had published the results of an investigation they had been making of current problems. Although the committee had no official status, their chairman had been appointed by the Prime Minister and the Chancellor of the Exchequer.

The Land Report was published in October 1913, and there was scarcely anything in the document with which Edwin Savill agreed. Angrily, he set to work and in the following January (jointly with Charles Adeane) published *The Land Retort*; it is subtitled: *A study of the land question with an answer to the report of the secret committee of enquiry.* He called it 'secret' because the committee had sat in private and had failed to disclose the sources of much of their evidence including the names of the witnesses. He complained that the members all belonged to the same political party; that except for their chairman no one of them was engaged in agriculture or knew anything about it; that in a purely partisan spirit they had established to their satisfaction what they had intended to establish; that the report was full of inaccuracies; that the committee had only cited evidence favourable to their points of view:

The proposals they bring forward ... are revolutionary and completely subversive of the present system of land tenure in this country. . . . To found legislation on evidence so partial would be unprecedented and dangerous. . . . The report contains a mass of unsound argument worked up by evidence carefully chosen; and on this flimsy basis the committee stand as the champions of the distressed agricultural industry. Our purpose in writing this book is to bring forward on behalf of agriculture some of those truths which have been so carefully suppressed.

After this promising opening the authors dealt with, and sought to demolish, nearly every finding and recommendation *The Report* contained. The committee had ranged over a wide field, and the following are only a few of the matters which were the subject of their 'subversive proposals'. The terms of employment and the wages of the agricultural labourer; his health and education; his housing and the age-old controversy of the tied cottage; his access to land for his own cultivation and the alleged failure of the Small Holdings and Allotments Act of 1907 ('two acres and a cow') to make them available to the right people; the case for establishing 'wage tribunals' and 'land courts'; the alleged insecurity of the tenant farmer; the deficiencies of the rating system; the alleged under-cultivation of the soil and the reasons for it; the breaking up of great estates and the reasons for that.

Again and again the joint authors of *The Retort* denied the facts as stated, accused the committee of exaggeration, or if there was hardship prescribed remedies of their own.

Whether, and if so to what extent, the recommendations of the committee of enquiry would have been embodied in subsequent legislation will never be known. Things had been happening in the meantime, vital to the future of the nation and possibly to its survival. In the light of them these domestic issues, important though they were, paled almost into insignificance. The faggots were piled high; the train had been laid, the assassins at Sarajevo applied the match; the inevitable conflagration followed.

On 4 August 1914 Great Britain declared war on Germany.

5

Family interlude

*Three more Savill brothers: Lydall (Gen. IX, 1894–
1940), Eric (b. 1895), Alfred Cecil (1897–1943) – the
Kemps – halcyon days in The Wilderness – King Edward
the peacemaker – memories of an early twentieth-century
upbringing – Bleriot – Scott in the Antarctic –
the Titanic – gathering clouds – Savills at the Front in
the First World War*

We saw earlier that Alfred Savill (Gen. VII, 1829–1905) had five
sons by his wife, *née* Eleanor Hallings Smith. The first was
christened Alfred after his father; the second was Arthur Edward,
who became a solicitor; the third and fourth were Edwin and
Robert Cecil; the fifth was Henry Norman. The firm had been
renamed 'Afred Savill and Sons' by the time of old Alfred's death,
and three of his sons, Alfred, Edwin and Norman, were already
firmly established in partnership. Although in 1905 the head
office of the firm was at 39 New Broad Street, in the City of
London, its practice was still largely agricultural. The young men
had been born and bred on the soil and trained by their father.
There can have been little about contemporary methods and the
economics of farming in England and Wales they did not know
between them.

Alfred, the eldest son (Gen. VIII, 1854–1928), had married in
1882 Augusta, daughter of Frederick Washington of Hackney,
by whom he had two daughters, Gwendolen and Vera. Edwin
(1868–1947), whose activities in opposing the People's Budget we
described in the last chapter, had married in 1893 Helen Webster,
a daughter of Alexander Davidson Kemp of Chigwell, by whom
he had three sons and one daughter. Norman (1874–1945) had
married (first) Jane, daughter of Charles Crofton Black of

74

Buckhurst Hill, by whom he had two daughters, Margaret and Nancy.*

Edwin's wife, like his grandmother Maria Lydall, was a personality. Both in their ways had much to contribute to the Savill strain. Helen's mother, Anne Kemp, had been a temperamental, self-willed lady who died at 49 from pneumonia contracted as a result of rising prematurely from childbed to attend a political meeting. But by that time she had had fourteen children to whom she bequeathed her temperament, aquiline nose, heavy jowl, and to twelve of them her red hair.

Alexander Kemp, who had inflated ideas about his lineage, was strongly opposed to his daughter's proposed marriage. Edwin's father was a builder and for a Kemp to marry into 'trade', as had a Lydall two generations earlier, would be derogatory. This attitude, adopted by the Kemps generally, brought the entire Savill family into defensive action. The Savills constantly quarrelled among themselves, but they closed their ranks and stood shoulder to shoulder if any one of them was attacked from outside. It was one of those occasions. Edwin was told in the hearing of the enemy he 'must be *mad* to want to marry one of those red-haired Kemps'. His elder brother, Arthur, added for good measure: 'All red-haired women stink of fox.'

Helen happened to have brown hair, but Cecily, her daughter, wrote in an affectionate memoir: 'I am bound to say that my mother, though odourless, had a red-haired temperament.' She was also endowed with high intelligence, a keen sense of fun, and a talent for landscape gardening which in a woman of that period was remarkable.

Edwin's three sons were all destined to enter the family business. They were Generation IX. Edwin Lydall was born on 20 February 1894; Eric Humphrey on 20 October 1895; Alfred Cecil on 22 December 1897. They were all educated at Malvern, whence Lydall went on to Wye College. Eric, after the end of the First World War, took a degree in agriculture at Magdalene

*For Norman Savill's second marriage, see page 155.

College, Cambridge. Alfred (the third in three successive generations of Savills to bear that name) went from Malvern into the
Regular Army. Helen Cecily, born 27 February 1905, was the
youngest of the family.

Edwin and Helen Savill, probably to escape the strictures of
their respective relations, spent the first year of their married
life in London. When Lydall was born they went to live in
Upminster; he was a delicate child and it was thought the country
air would do him good. Then Eric and Alfred were born, and
in 1900 they moved again – this time to Frimley Green in Surrey.
None of the boys was very strong and the doctors considered
gravel soil preferable to Essex clay.

The Wilderness was a biggish house even before Edwin built
on to it. It was bounded on one side by the Basingstoke canal,
Frimley lock was opposite, and the towpath ran in front of its
windows. On the other side of the canal was a wide expanse of
heath and woodland, mainly birch and Scots pine. A leat from
the canal – known as 'the brook' – flowed through the garden
and was overhung by pollard willows. It would be hard to
imagine more idyllic surroundings in which to bring up a family
of young children.

They learned the lore of the countryside, and to ride and fish
and shoot. They played brigands and climbed trees. But most of
their holidays were spent by the water, mud up to their knees –
catching tadpoles, setting eel traps, messing about with leaky old
boats. What fun to dare your younger brother to make his way
precariously along the top of the lock gates, secure in the knowledge that if he fell in, the lock-keeper would fish him out! There
were horses and ponies and dogs; Cecily's donkey; Eric's guinea
fowl; families of dormice living among the tree roots; water rats;
dragonflies; stilted herons at dawn; cerulean flash of a kingfisher
in the noon sunshine . . . halcyon days indeed.

But the halcyon days of the ancients were short lived.* They
ended abruptly; so, alas, did these. In 1911 the children's parents

*In Greek mythology the halcyon was a bird, possibly resembling a king-
fisher, who built her nest upon the sea. There she laid and hatched her eggs.

separated. Edwin, who had formed an attachment to another lady, left Frimley and took a flat in London. Later the couple moved to Hertfordshire and remained together until his death in 1947.

Helen Savill rented a small house near Chobham, and thenceforth the four children spent occasional holidays with their father and the rest of the time with their mother. She supplemented a modest income by exercising professionally her skill as a landscape gardener. Farewell to The Wilderness – friendly old house; to the heath and woodlands; to the shimmering water; to the lock and its lock-keeper; to the brook beneath the pollard willows. Worst of all, farewell to that family unity, and consequent security, which are cornerstones of children's happiness.

In 1901, when Queen Victoria died, Lydall had been aged 7 Eric 5, Alfred not yet 4. None of them was old enough to share in the universal sense of personal loss. Nor were they old enough to share in the national anxiety when the coronation of her son, King Edward VII, fixed for 26 June 1902, had perforce to be abandoned at two days' notice. Crowned heads of their heirs from all over Europe, presidents of overseas republics, Indian princes, representatives of our dominions and colonies, had assembled in London to attend a ceremony of unparalleled magnificence. The King had turned 60 and for some time there had been rumours, officially denied, about his state of health. Then on 24 June, two days before Coronation Day, it was announced that he was suffering from appendicitis. Everything had to be put off. An operation was performed the same morning, and mercifully during the ensuing weeks the royal patient made a steady recovery. The postponed coronation, its ritual shortened but its splendour undimmed, took place on 9 August.

Nor in the early years of the twentieth century were the young Savills old enough to appreciate the niceties of the new king's

---

'Halcyon days' were a period of fourteen days' peace and calm while she reared her brood.

relationships with foreign rulers; his cosmopolitan temperament; his tact; the tolerant attitude he adopted towards his ministers; the popularity he enjoyed among his people at all social levels. When Prince of Wales he had been interested in housing. As Duke of Cornwall he owned many streets of small houses in South London, and he was also a model landlord at Sandringham. We mentioned earlier that the report of the Royal Commission on the Housing of the Working Classes, appointed in 1884, stirred the public conscience. The Prince, at his own request, had been one of the commissioners, and the only speech he ever made as a peer in the House of Lords was on that subject. He said: 'I take the keenest and liveliest interest in this great question.'

King Edward VII was not clever, but he was a man with a keen sense of responsibility. He earned his title 'the peace-maker' not by political astuteness or diplomatic initiative; rather by an innate faith in the blessings of peace and a revulsion at the thought of war. Above all, he was human – a man who enjoyed life to the full, wanted others to enjoy it and endeared himself to most, if not all, his subjects by his human frailties and peccadillos.

But that is not to imply that in this comparatively peaceful prewar period there were no excitements. Three outstanding events during the adolescence of the Savills will remain always in their memories and in those of their contemporaries. The first was pure achievement; the second, achievement marred by tragedy; the third was tragedy, stark and unrelieved.

On 5 July 1909 the French aviator, Louis Blériot, flew across the Straits of Dover in a monoplane having a wing span of twenty-four feet powered by a twenty-four-horsepower three-cylinder engine. The distance is twenty-three miles and it took him about half an hour. It is difficult for the younger generation, in this age of Concorde, to imagine the excitement which this feat by Blériot created. Yet it was tinged by apprehension. It was recognized that the possibility of a man, or men, being transported from one country to another *by air* weakened for ever the natural defences of our island fortress.

Captain Robert Falcon Scott and his four gallant companions,

Dr E. R. Wilson, Captain Lawrence Oates, Lieutenant H. R. Bowers and Petty Officer Edgar Evans, had reached the South Pole on 17 January of the same year, although the British public did not learn about it until afterwards. On arriving at the Pole, after surmounting immense difficulties, they found Amundsen's tent. Amundsen was the Norwegian explorer who had been racing them, and here was evidence that he had got there first. In the tent was a message addressed to Scott recording that the Norwegians had gained their objective on 14 December and had left three days later. The finding of the tent in the Antarctic waste was a tribute to the competence of Bowers, the surveyor member of the British team; a subsequent recalculation of his observations showed that his error in determining the polar position, if any, had been negligible.

Philosophic, but disappointed, Scott and his party started on the return journey. The weather was dreadful and the difficulties they encountered were even more formidable than on the way out. Frostbite made marching slow and painful, and through some disastrous accident they lost a large part of their limited supply of precious oil. However, fair progress was made to the head of the Beardmore Glacier, which they reached on 7 February. At that point Petty Officer Evans broke under the strain; that delayed them and he died ten days later.

The other four pressed on, and the next victim was Captain Oates. He was too frostbitten to continue and became conscious that he was becoming a drag on the others. In the hope that they might yet save their lives, he resolved to end his own. On 17 March he undid the flap of the tent, turned towards his leader and said: 'I'm just going outside; I may be some time. . . .' Oates went out into the blizzard and was not seen again.

On 29 March Scott made the final entry in his journal: 'We shall stick it out to the end, but we are getting weaker, of course, and the end cannot be far. It seems a pity, but I do not think I can write any more.'

A relief party with dog teams that had set out from the base to meet Scott was held up by a blizzard in early March and forced to return owing to a shortage of dog food. Eight months later a search party found the tent and the bodies. Scott's journal, letters, photographs and a message to the public were recovered; they have been described gloriously as 'part of the heritage of the nation'.

The sinking of RMS *Titanic* on her maiden voyage, during the night of 14-15 April in the same year, was an appalling shock on both sides of the Atlantic. She was the biggest ship in the world and her appointments were the most glamorous. Although no one dreamed of the possibility of shipwreck, it had been claimed that because of her unique construction (a double bottom and sixteen watertight compartments separated by massive transverse bulkheads) she was unsinkable. Distinguished people, including many rich Americans, had vied with one another to secure passages; John Jacob Astor, the multi-millionaire, was among those drowned. The ship had a tremendous send-off from Southampton, and an even more tumultuous welcome awaited her in New York. The master of the *Titanic*, Captain Edward J. Smith, was the senior captain of the White Star Line. He was due for retirement and this was to be his last voyage; alas, it *was* his last voyage, for in the tradition of the sea he went down with his ship.

On 14 April at 11.40 p.m., somewhere south of Cape Race, the *Titanic* struck an iceberg. It was a glancing blow but sufficient to rip open a section of the starboard side of her hull, wrecking the bulkheads and flooding the forward compartments. Most of the passengers felt the impact, but initially few realized that anything serious had happened. Those who had gone to bed early turned over and went to sleep again; games and conversation in the public rooms were resumed; the ship's band continued to play ragtime. The passengers were told they had 'grazed' an iceberg and some of them went to collect the curiously shaped bits of ice that had showered upon her decks.

One of the passengers was Mr Thomas Andrews, managing director of Harland and Wolff of Belfast who had built the ship; he was called into consultation immediately. After an inspection

MARIA SAVILL (*née* LYDALL)
1807–1894
'builder employing twenty men'
Painted by Samuel Bellin

ALFRED SAVILL

1829–1905

of Chigwell Hall

ALFRED SAVILL
1854–1928

SIR EDWIN SAVILL OBE
1868–1947
President of the Surveyors' Institution 1924–5

his report was horrifying. With three of her watertight compartments flooded, she might stay afloat; with five flooded and the sea cascading over the tops of the bulkheads into the others, she was doomed.

Within moments of the impact the engines slowed down and stopped. The vibration everyone had got used to since leaving Southampton ceased, and there followed an uncanny stillness. Passengers, some of them in dressing gowns, came out of their cabins to find out what was happening; the public rooms began to empty, and the little knots of people chatting and joking in the long corridors failed to notice the scarcely perceptible tilt towards the bow. It was very cold outside, a clear starlight night with no moon, and that tiresome iceberg was no longer visible. Someone suggested it had chipped off some of their new paint and that the captain was unwilling to go on until it had been touched up; they would soon be under way again and in the meantime there was nothing to worry about.

'*All passengers on deck wearing lifebelts!*' Even then, few passengers realized there was any imminent danger; it was a routine precaution no doubt. But they hastened to obey, and on gaining the deck watched with interest while seamen took the canvas covers off the lifeboats. Not until the firing of the first rocket – soaring up, up, up into the darkness to explode and descend in a myriad of stars – did they grasp the dreadful truth. Rockets fired from a ship at night have only one meaning. Below, the band was still playing.

There were sixteen lifeboats and four collapsible rafts. Women and children were ordered into the boats first, but some of the women declined to leave their husbands. That was only one reason why some of the boats were lowered half-full. Another explanation is that this was done deliberately, the seamen in charge of the boats having been told to stand by to pick up more passengers to be passed down to them from the cargo ports. Whatever the explanation, it is indisputable that some of the boats got away without their full complement while others were overloaded. Once the women and children had been got on board, or were

81

thought to be on board, it was the men's turn; but many passengers of both sexes and a larger proportion of the crew were unable to secure accommodation either in boats or on rafts. They had two alternatives: one to jump into the sea and swim for it, the other to stay on deck until the waves engulfed them. The occupants of the lifeboats, as they pushed off, were told to row as far as possible from the ship to escape the suction when she went down.

She sank at 2.20 a.m., and the following is a contemporary account by an eyewitness who was in one of the lifeboats:

As we gazed awe-struck, she tilted slowly up, revolving apparently about a centre of gravity just astern of amidships until she attained a vertically upright position, and there she remained motionless.... Then, first sinking back a little at the stern, I thought, she slid down slowly through the water and dived slanting down.*

For quite a long time afterwards the air was filled with the heart-rending cries of people struggling in the icy water, and there are splendid stories of how some of the overcrowded boats, taking the risk of capsizing, went to their rescue. There were other stories.

The *Titanic* was equipped with wireless, a comparatively new invention. The wireless operator, from the moment of impact until she sank, remained in his cabin making distress signals. The first to respond was the Cunarder *Carpathia*, fifty-eight miles distant; she wirelessed back, 'Coming hard'. Her progress was slow because of an ice field, but she arrived on the scene at about 4 a.m. A few hours later she had taken on board all the survivors who were in the *Titanic*'s lifeboats or on the rafts. There is no record of anyone in the water being saved.

Needless to say, there were governmental and other inquiries both in England and in the United States. They continued for some years. Various suggestions were made about the basic causes of the catastrophe, but not all of them were substantiated. On one matter, however, there was no room for doubt. The Board of

*Lawrence Beesley, *The Loss of SS Titanic*, 1912.

Trade Regulations for the provision of life-saving equipment (they were later revised), which the White Star Line had complied with, were woefully inadequate. The sixteen lifeboats and four collapsible rafts had a maximum capacity of 1178 persons. The passengers and crew of the *Titanic* numbered 2207. Of this total 1635 were drowned. And that, very briefly, is the story of the greatest civil maritime disaster in the history of mankind.

In the meantime, on 6 May 1910, King Edward VII had died after a short illness. He was succeeded by his eldest surviving son, King George V, who was crowned in June of the following year. We noted earlier that at about this time the Liberals won two general elections in succession, and that their Parliament Act of 1911 had greatly reduced the powers of the House of Lords.

Nothing of much moment occurred at home during the next three years. Members of the House of Commons received payment for the first time; there was a railway strike; national insurance was introduced. But there was unrest abroad. A second Morocco crisis between Germany and France was resolved by compromise. The outbreak of a Balkan war was more ominous; it ended with the Treaty of Bucharest, under which most of Turkey-in-Europe was divided among the Balkan states.

Then, in 1914, like the outbreak of a thunderstorm that has been threatening for some time, came the First World War. Its immediate cause was the assassination of the Archduke, Francis Ferdinand, heir to the Austrian throne, at Sarajevo on 28 July. Austria resolved to avenge this outrage by securing political control over Serbia, if need be by force of arms. Russia and France were unwilling to see Serbia humiliated and Russia mobilized. Germany, allied to Austria, failed to restrain her and Austria declared war. Germany, sensing that a European war was now inevitable, sought to gain the maximum military advantage by declaring war, first on Russia and then on France. Great Britain declared war on 4 August when the Germans over-ran Belgium.

But the basic causes of the First World War went much deeper. Fundamentally, they stemmed from the empire-building policy pursued by Germany after the victorious conclusion of the Franco-Prussian War in 1871 and the creation within her frontiers of powerfully armed states menacing Austria, Russia and the defeated France. The international situation became one of alarm and mutual distrust, which Bismarck, fearing an explosion, did his best to contain. But the Kaiser grew impatient and dismissed Bismarck; his dismissal prompted the drawing by Bernard Partridge, 'Dropping the Pilot', one of the most famous political cartoons ever to appear in *Punch*. Armaments went on piling up, and before long the new Germany had become the greatest military power in Europe. Disarmament conferences at TheHague between 1909 and 1912 were as inconclusive as such conferences tend to be. Germany's undisguised ambition to dominate and expand, her thinly veiled threats, her extensive naval building programme, the Kaiser's inflammatory speeches – all these things combined to lead other countries, including ourselves, to believe that Germany would not hesitate to go to war if she thought she could thereby achieve her aims. The opportunity had arisen and she decided to do so.

One difference between the outbreak of the First World War in 1914 and the second in 1939 was the attitude of the man and woman in the street. In 1914 we experienced a surfeit of emotional jingoism, of cheering and singing and waving of flags. Even in small towns there were ceremonial military parades, and marching and counter-marching to the beat of drums. Field Marshal Earl Kitchener was Minister for War; before conscription, which was to be introduced later, there can have been few hoardings whence a portrait of the Field Marshal did not glare down on passers-by. He pointed an accusing finger: 'Your King and Country need you' was his message. And irresponsible young women roamed the West End of London tendering a white feather to any young man who was not in uniform. The possibility that he had volunteered, and was bitterly disappointed at having been turned down for medical reasons, never entered their silly minds.

The two elder Savills joined up immediately. Lydall was 20, Eric 18, and they both enlisted in the University and Public

Schools Corps as privates. Lydall was shortly commissioned in the South Staffordshire Regiment and sent to France, but he had always been delicate and the rigours of trench warfare proved too much for him. He was invalided out of the Army in 1915, and after a short spell with a country land agent went into his father's office in London.

Eric was commissioned in the Devon Regiment in the same year, and by 1916 had been promoted captain. He was gravely wounded on the Somme in 1916, and was awarded the Military Cross. His recovery took two years and he was returned to his unit for the last few months of the war.

The circumstances of his wound merit retelling. The battalion, engaged in a night attack on 'High Wood' on 20 July, was advancing in open order when an enemy bullet through his left shoulder severed the sub-clavian artery; by chance the business end of the artery was compressed between broken ends of the clavicle, which saved him from bleeding to death. He was only 500 yards from the enemy front line and lay in a corn field for more than seventeen hours. Then he was spotted by Private Veale, who came out to his rescue and managed to drag him into a shell hole. Veale went back for water and returned with two volunteers, one of whom was shot dead; because of heavy fire, on Eric Savill's orders, he was left in another shell hole. At dusk, accompanied by more volunteers, Veale made a further attempt and repelled the advance of an enemy patrol with a machine gun. Eventually they got the semi-conscious young man to comparative safety. 'For most conspicuous bravery' Private Theodore William Henry Veale, of the Devon Regiment, was awarded the Victoria Cross.

In August 1914 Alfred, the youngest of the three boys, had just left Malvern and was awaiting the result of his examination for the Regular Army, which he had taken during his last term. At that time there were two main entries. One was through the Royal Military Academy, Woolwich (commonly called 'The Shop'), and the other through the Royal Military College, Sandhurst. To join the Royal Engineers or the Royal Artillery, considered the brains of the Army, the entry was through The Shop for which the examination was harder.

Alfred's passing into The Shop was announced in September 1914, and a year later, when only 17, he was commissioned in the Royal Field Artillery. Like his two brothers, he was sent to France. First he commanded a battery in the Welsh Division, and later in the 57th West Lancs. Division. He was gassed and wounded, was three times mentioned in despatches, and won the Military Cross and Bar. When, still aged only 19, Major Savill was invested at Buckingham Palace, he was said to be the youngest major in the British Army. In 1919 he retired to the Regular Army Reserve of Officers; presently we shall record the distinguished military service rendered by Lieutenant-Colonel Alfred Savill DSO, MC in the Second World War.*

*See page 132.

6

1914–18: 'War to end Wars'

*Maintaining a practice – London managements – the
Company of Leathersellers – leasehold enfranchisement –
on valuers and valuing – Edwin Savill at the Home
Front – zeppelins – commandeering and compensation –
war damage and compensation for that – rent restrictions –
intensive food production*

But for the outbreak of war, Edwin's two eldest sons, Lydall and
Eric, would shortly have joined the family firm. Since the death
of old Alfred (Gen. VII) in 1905 it had continued to expand. This
was due to the efforts of all three partners, but especially to
Edwin's. He is said to have been lazy at Uppingham, where he
went from Chigwell grammar School, but once in his father's
office he had shown a flair for business and a capacity for hard
work, and had taken a keen interest in everything relevant to his
profession. His elder brother, Alfred, the senior partner, and his
younger brother, Norman, were mainly interested in the management of agricultural land and in matters arising from it; had they
been left to themselves, the practice of Alfred Savill and Sons
would probably have gone on developing on those lines.

Edwin was the first of the Savills to concern himself with the
growth of an urban practice as much as of a country practice.
He took an active part in the affairs of the Surveyors' Institution,
where he read papers and led discussions on important contemporary issues; and as vice-chairman of the Land Union he made
a name for himself both in the Institution and elsewhere. In 1906
the office moved from New Broad Street to 24 Great Winchester
Street, also in the City of London. Edwin made contacts in the
City and outside it, and gradually the firm came to be known,

87

no longer principally as agricultural surveyors and valuers, but as valuers of all classes of property for a wide variety of purposes. They included valuations of land and buildings for sale and purchase, lettings, mortgages, insurance, the assessment of compensation for compulsory acquisitions, and so forth. Since his time, owing to a continuous spate of legislation affecting land, the scope of a valuer in general practice has been considerably widened. Today it includes the making of valuations for the enfranchisement of leaseholds, capital gains tax, capital transfer tax, the discharge or modification of restrictive covenants under the Law of Property Acts; and valuers will soon be making valuations for the purpose of development land tax.

We remarked earlier that a skilled professional valuer must be in the market. By 'in the market' we mean actively engaged in buying and selling on behalf of clients – not standing at a corner of the market square observing the goings-on through a spy glass. That applies to the valuation of every saleable commodity. It stands to reason. A man requiring a valuation of an antique teapot would be well advised to consult a firm which from day to day buys and sells antique teapots; of a block of shares, a stockbroker; of his wine, a wine merchant. For a professional valuer the 'higgle of the market' is the best of all schools. The tastes of the public are notoriously capricious and fashions change for no apparent reason. A valuer who is constantly in the market can often sense and anticipate changes. 'Fashion, though Folly's child, and guide of fools, rules e'en the wisest.' And fashion can create, or destroy, values.

Edwin Savill was aware of this, and so were his partners. It was a period when some of the most distinguished firms of surveyors and valuers, whose names were household words, were self-conscious about the buying and selling of property for clients – especially the latter. They did so, if only because it was lucrative, but with an uncomfortable feeling that it was 'unprofessional'. Alfred Savill and Sons had no inhibitions of that kind. From the early years of the century they had made it known that they were not merely willing, but eager, to buy and sell properties on commission. They claimed to be good valuers; that was how the partners had learned their jobs as valuers, and would go on learning it, all their lives.

During this prewar period the number of the firm's managements, still the mainstay of its business, had increased considerably. The management of urban estates was a new department and two managements, introduced and undertaken personally by Edwin Savill, were sufficiently important to deserve mention. The Eyre estate was in St John's Wood. The other, mainly in the City but also dotted about the inner suburbs, belonged to the Worshipful Company of Leathersellers.

The Eyre estate was developed by the Eyre family during the nineteenth century. It is bounded on the north by Swiss Cottage, on the west by Abbey Road, on the east by Avenue Road, and on the south by Wellington Place adjoining Lord's cricket ground. There were at that time a few properties outside this broad area, which amounts in total to about 120 acres. Edwin, surveyor and steward, maintained a local estate office in St John's Wood under an assistant steward who collected the rents and undertook day-to-day routine jobs such as the assessment dilapidations. Sales, relettings and estate policy were under the direction of Edwin and his staff in the head office. At about that time the firm established an architectural and building surveyors' department. Before the First World War most of the Eyre Estate was ground-rented. Many of the ground leases have since fallen in, and the sites of the old Victorian houses have been redeveloped. One of the most interesting developments, in the Finchley Road, is the block of flats known as Eyre Court; the architects, Messrs T. P. Bennett and Son, claim that Eyre Court was the first large block of flats in Inner London to have a forecourt big enough for the tenants to park their cars within the curtilage.

The 'Mistery or Art of the Leathersellers of the City of London' dates from the thirteenth century, when there is evidence of a fraternity of Tanners and White Tawyers.* In 1372 'men of the

---

*'Tawyers' were persons who made hide into leather without using tannin, especially by soaking it in a solution of alum and salt.

Mistery of Leathersellers', jointly with the Craft of Pursers,★ presented a Bill to the City Corporation desiring regulations to prevent fraudulent dealings in the dyeing or staining of inferior grades of leather, which were being passed off in the trade 'for other than it was in deceit of the people'. The Bill was granted by the Mayor and Court of Aldermen and supervisors were appointed.

By 1444 the Leathersellers were constituted the legal authority, with power of search, for inspecting and approving all leather and wares made of leather throughout the country. That was by virtue of a Charter of Incorporation granted by King Henry VI. A second charter was granted by Queen Elizabeth I in 1559, and a third by King James I in 1604. An Act of Parliament in the same year defined 'leather' as follows: 'The skins and hides of Ox, Bull, Cow, Calf, Deer, red and fallow, Goats and Sheep, being tanned or tawed, and every salt hide is, shall be, and ever hath been, reputed and taken for Leather.' The time had not yet come when it was necessary specifically to exclude, by statutory provision, a variety of synthetic substitutes known compendiously as 'plastic'.

The company had possessed five earlier Halls, the first on land north of the City and abutting on the City Wall. In 1540 the wardens and court began looking for larger premises, and among the religious houses lately dissolved by King Henry VIII was a convent called the Priory of the Black Nuns of St Helen. The buildings were in the ward of Bishopsgate and adjoined St Helen's church. They had been granted by the King to Sir Richard Cromwell, from whom, after prolonged negotiations, they were acquired by the Leathersellers. Collectively, the estate was known as Little St Helen's; but the close to the south of the parishioners' side of St Helen's church was known, as now, as Great St Helen's.

In 1941 the fifth Hall was seriously damaged by enemy action

★'Pursers' were makers of leather purses.

and much of the contents destroyed. The sixth and present Hall and premises were completed in 1959, the reception room having been designed by the late Mr Louis de Soissons RA, and the livery hall and the rest of the rooms by his partner, Mr Kenneth Peacock FRIBA.

Today the hub of the estate is St Helen's Place, which runs through from Bishopsgate to St Mary Axe. It has an area of about two acres and is fully developed with offices. There were other estates belonging to the company originally under the firm's management. That in Copthall Avenue was later sold, and most of the ground-rented houses on an outlying estate near Barnet have been enfranchised under the provisions of the Leasehold Reform Act 1967. In spite of these curtailments the Leathersellers' estate is still extensive, besides being of great historic importance. At the time of writing Richard Webster OBE is surveyor to the company.

The Leasehold Reform Act 1967, passed by the then Labour government, applies to dwelling houses (not flats) held on 'long leases' (i.e. not less than twenty-one years) when the ground rent does not exceed two-thirds of the rateable value. It enables a sitting ground-lessee, qualified by no more than five years' occupation, compulsorily to acquire the freehold interest from the reversioner at a price based on site value only. The intention was to protect the lessee from the loss of his capital in the shape of bricks and mortar when the lease expired. The government, however, overlooked the fact that the sitting lessee is rarely the lessee who built the house. In any case, he should have amortized his capital by means of a sinking fund which, if he purchased the leasehold interest, should have been allowed for in the purchase price.

It is an elementary planning principle that when the properties comprising an urban estate are worn out, and the ground leases fall in, the estate should be redeveloped as a whole. That applies whether the landowner is a private person, the freeholder of a great estate like Eyre, Grosvenor or Cadogan, a corporate body like the Leathersellers' Company, or a local authority. But if in the meantime the estate has been broken up into a multiplicity of small freeholds, separately owned, comprehensive redevelopment is impossible – even by a local authority armed with powers of compulsory acquisition. It is to be feared that as the years go by, owing to this short-sighted piece of legislation, much of our great architectural heritage will be lost to us.

During the First World War the national watchword, whenever and wherever it could be made to apply, was 'business as usual'. There was no officially sponsored scheme for evacuation, and most people who lived in London or in other big cities elected to stay put. The same with business and industry. It was exceptional for a firm established, say, in London, to move its office or factory outside. As in the Second World War, there was a shortage of building materials and an even greater shortage of labour. It prevented, so long as the war lasted, almost every form of building except for purposes of the war effort; the most a landowner or his agent could do was to keep his properties in reasonable repair.

In the First World War, as in the Second, the normal business of surveyors and estate agents declined, but it was replaced by a variety of abnormal activities – some of them irksome and none very lucrative. Transactions in some categories of real estate fell by more than half, though it is recorded that during the first three weeks after the declaration on 4 August 1914 the property market was buoyant. The Stock Exchange was closed.

Edwin Savill was not long in getting the first of his war jobs. Within a few weeks he was appointed by the War Office to assess compensation to landowners in Essex and Suffolk for loss of or damage to properties as a result of their being commandeered in connection with the defence of London from air attack.

In 1914 aerial warfare was in its infancy and the Royal Flying Corps had only been formed in 1912. The Germans were more advanced than we were, and had great hopes of their fleet of zeppelins. In the event, those hopes were not fulfilled and all the later raids on this country were by aeroplanes – which did considerably more damage.

The zeppelin, an airship, had been invented by Count Ferdinand von Zeppelin in 1900 and was called after him. It was made of aluminium and consisted of a number of compartments each containing a bag of gas. The airship was slow-moving and unwieldy and when caught in our searchlights resembled a long, thin silver cigar. To begin with, we relied on an artillery barrage for our defence; later, however, the zeppelin was found to be more vulnerable to fighter planes, most of them single-seaters, which attacked it with machine guns or bombed it from above. The gas was hydrogen and highly inflammable; once alight, the destruction of the airship followed inevitably. Those old enough to have experienced the zeppelin raids will recall the mounting excitement when a zeppelin, flying at great height, was seen to be surrounded by our shell bursts. Suddenly one end of the tiny cylindrical object began to glow, and moments later it was ablaze its entire length; then it tipped and appeared to pause for a few seconds before the raging inferno plunged to earth. A roar of applause arose from London. The first zeppelin we brought down was in July 1915 over Ghent; and the first in England, soon afterwards, at Cuffley in Hertfordshire. A number of others were destroyed later. Edwin's job was to value the land taken for use as sites for our batteries and flying fields.

The bulk of the work in the firm's London office was the assessment and negotiation of compensation payable to clients under two heads. The first, under the Defence of the Realm Acts, was for land taken over by government departments – most of it by the War Office Lands Branch and the Ministry of Munitions. The second was for damage caused by enemy action.

The area commandeered on behalf of the Crown was soon considerable. By the end of 1916 it amounted to 150,000 acres, plus buildings having an annual value of £2½ million. Compensation claims by its dispossessed owners were made under the first of the Defence of the Realm Acts. The Act of 1916 provided for the release of the land when the war ended or within a limited period afterwards, or for its compulsory acquisition. The compensating authority on behalf of all departments was the newly formed War Losses Commission. The 1916 Act also contained provisions designed to safeguard the Crown against losses it might otherwise incur as a result of buildings erected on the land during the war, some containing valuable machinery, reverting to the original owners. Towards the end of the war the War Losses Commission, overburdened with work, called in two expert valuers to assist them. One was Edwin Savill.

The basis of compensation for damage by enemy action was a matter of acute controversy from the late autumn of 1914, when German warships appeared on the horizon and shelled the Hartle-pools, Whitby and Scarborough. It was our first experience of what by the standards of the 1914–18 war was extensive damage to property and grave injury to the civilian population. Initially, there was no right to compensation unless the victim was insured, and the insurance was voluntary. A landlord was under no obligation to insure; nor was his tenant, though the fact that his premises had suffered war damage did not exempt him from the repairing covenants in his lease or tenancy agreement. The War Risks Insurance Committee were appointed to administer the scheme and resolve anomalies, while the State Insurance Office had responsibility for the business side including finance.

London and the Eastern Counties were considered the most vulnerable parts of the country, and most of the inhabitants joined the scheme if they could afford to. Few who lived in the more remote parts of the United Kingdom – e.g. Devon and Cornwall – bothered. The many opponents of the voluntary insurance scheme were headed by a body, called the War Damage Committee, under the chairmanship of the Lord Mayor of Norwich. The committee contended that the scheme was unfair to those who lived or worked in the vulnerable areas. They said it was, in effect, a special war tax imposed on one section of the public; and because they lived in places where the bombing was most frequent and their business constantly interrupted, they were the section who could least afford to bear it. The committee pointed to France, whose president had promised that everyone who suffered war damage would be compensated in full. They urged our government to follow that example, wipe out the insurance scheme, and undertake that every subject of the Crown who had suffered in this way could be fully compensated by the Exchequer.

The government were embarrassed by these criticisms and sought to compromise; for example, the premiums were reduced by half. But few regarded the concessions as acceptable, and it was not until long after the end of the war that the War Damage Committee achieved all they had been contending for. The meeting of all claims for compensation for war damage was to be one of Germany's liabilities under the Peace Treaty. In January 1920 all persons who had suffered in this respect were invited to submit claims or amended claims to the Reparation Commission of the Board of Trade, and local authorities were required to make this known in their areas. It remains to add that the claims were eventually met and compensation for war damage, in whole or in part, made previously from other public funds, was reimbursed.

1915 saw the passing of the first of the Rent Acts – that series of Acts of Parliament, frequently amended, that has continued until the present time. The prewar shortage of working-class houses had been made worse by the impossibility, under war conditions, of replacing those that were worn out or rendered uninhabitable; but more particularly by big shifts of population – for example, into the areas of the munition factories. The Rent and Mortgage Interest Restrictions Act 1915 applied to houses under a specified rateable value according to where they were situated. The prewar rent was frozen for the duration, plus increases in rates and a percentage of the cost of any improvements made by the landlord. The maximum rent, thus fixed, was called the 'standard rent'; the tenancy became known as a 'statutory tenancy'; the house as a 'controlled house'. Once, however, the landlord of a controlled house was able to regain possession as a result of his tenant vacating voluntarily (or, subject to conditions, on the death of the statutory tenant), it became decontrolled and there was no restriction on the rent chargeable to a new tenant.

In the country, after a myopic start, the necessity for changing our farming methods to increase the home production of food-stuffs, especially wheat, became recognized – but only gradually. To begin with, no change was made. Foreign purchases of cereals continued; farmers were content to go on producing milk, butter and cheese, root crops, and no more than their normal proportion of wheat. Before, however, the war had lasted a year, the rate of destruction of our shipping had begun to cause alarm. The government appointed a committee of agriculturists, under the chairmanship of Lord Milner, to examine the position and advise what steps should be taken to maintain and, if possible, increase 'the present production of food in England and Wales on the assumption that the war may be prolonged beyond the harvest of 1916'.

The Milner Committee reported, in July 1915, that the main objective must be more home-grown wheat. Their first recommendation, applauded vigorously by Edwin Savill (who had had much to say on this subject), was to encourage wheat-growing: farmers should be guaranteed a minimum price per quarter for at least four years. The committee recommended, secondly, that district committees should be appointed to ascertain in their districts the total acreage under plough and the areas under wheat, oats and potatoes, and lay down standards of endeavour. Thirdly, they recommended that each committee should examine and report on the capacity of the farms in their district and the willing-ness of the farmers to co-operate. Failing a good prospect of co-operation, the Milner Committee warned that consideration would have to be given to statutory compulsion.

Instead of acting on this advice at once, the government were dilatory. They set up district committees, but not all of them functioned efficiently. No steps were taken to implement the recommendation, so strongly supported by Savill, to guarantee the price of wheat. In the meantime, shipping losses increased until in April 1917 they became astronomic; the British Empire lost in one month 546447 gross tons out of world losses of 866616 gross tons. In April 1917 America had come into the war, outraged by the sinking of the *Lusitania*, and thereafter transport for the import of foodstuffs was in competition with that required for bringing men and munitions.

Another difficulty was the shortage of labour on the farms. More than a third of the population, normally employed on the land, had been called up to the armed forces or sent to work in munition factories. It was impracticable to get them back. Prisoners of war were put to work on the farms, women were recruited, and public-school boys were employed during their holidays.

In December 1917 the government, belatedly, implemented the main recommendations of the Milner Committee and took steps to introduce the measures of compulsion which hitherto they had shied from. As Lord Ernle put it:

In its general principles the policy of the plough was imposed on the agricultural industry by natural necessities. Broadly speaking, the country wanted the largest quantity of food in the shortest possible time. As between grass and tillage, the only question worth considering was by which system the greatest number of people could be provided with subsistence diet. To this there was only one answer. Arable farming feeds at least four times as many persons per acre as can be fed from grass of average quality.*

The Corn Production Act 1917, an emergency measure, was in four parts. Part I prescribed minimum prices for wheat and oats until 1922; Part II provided for a minimum wage for agricultural labourers; Part III placed conditional restrictions on the raising of farm rents; Part IV gave the government power to enforce efficient cultivation.

The minimum prices under Part I ranged from 60s. a quarter for wheat in 1917, to 45s. a quarter in 1922; for oats, from 38s. 6d. in 1917 to 24s. a quarter in 1922. Should the average price fall below the statutory minimum, the grower might claim from the Board of Agriculture a sum, in the case of wheat equal to

*English Farming, Past and Present, 6th edition, 1961.

four times, and in the case of oats five times, the difference between the average price and the minimum price in respect of every acre of wheat or oats produced. This guarantee of minimum prices was what Edwin Savill had been urging, if in slightly different form, ever since the outbreak of war.

Under Part II the minimum agricultural wage, normally, was to be 25s. a week; 'wages boards' were established to deal with exceptional cases. Part III provided that the rent of an agricultural holding, under any contract made or varied after the passing of the Act, should not exceed the rent that might have been obtained if the minimum prices laid down in Part I had not been in operation.

Part IV was highly controversial. In retrospect it may be thought only reasonable for the government, having protected the grower from any risk of loss, to have required him to put his land to the best possible use. There was power to enforce proper cultivation, and in an extreme case, where a farmer failed to farm to the required standard, to evict him and take over his land. Responsibility for enforcement was entrusted to new 'county agricultural executive committees', who had powers of delegation in this and other matters to the district committees. And they, in turn, formed subcommittees to deal with such matters as surveys, supplies, labour and finance.

Edwin Savill was a member of the Advisory Committee to the Board of Agriculture, the Advisory Committee to the Timber Controller, and the National Service Advisory Committee. For his public work in these capacities he was awarded the OBE in 1918 and a knighthood in 1921.

It remains to record that during the year 1917 about a million acres were added to the total of arable land in the United Kingdom; that the production of white corn in 1917 exceeded that in 1914, 1915 and 1916 by 4,710,000 quarters, 3,837,000 quarters and 5,827,000 quarters respectively; that the weight of roots and hay produced in 1917 also exceeded that in any of the three previous years. Another notable achievement during 1917 and 1918 was an increase in the number of allotments from 530,000 to 1,400,000.

Victory in November 1918 was mainly thanks to the gallantry and endurance of our soldiers, sailors and airmen; but it was also due to the efforts of our farmers, without which we might never have gained it. There were times when we had to tighten our belts and it was touch-and-go, but we survived.

7

Professional interlude

*Veterans of the staff – George Eve (1879–1959) – Daisy,
the underbidder – Sir Edwin Savill, President of the
Surveyors' Institution, 1924 – changes in the firm –
surprising effect of a half-bottle of port – Sir Eric Savill
and the Savill Garden in Windsor Great Park*

Edwin Savill was so occupied with his war work that he had little
time to devote to the practice of Alfred Savill and Sons. His
service on advisory committees involved more than just attending
meetings; he was essentially a man who liked to go and see things
for himself. He also found time to give addresses and write
articles. In the *Transactions* of his professional society, the Surveyors' Institution, are a number of contributions on the occupation and use of land under war conditions. As a valuer, he was
concerned with compensation and a paper, 'Some notes on the
Defence of the Realm (Acquisition of land) Act 1916', is analytical
and constructive.

Norman Savill, too, had a wartime job in the office of the
National Savings movement; so it was that responsibility for
keeping the business going devolved mainly on their elder brother
Alfred, who had now turned 60. He had the help of his nephew,
Lydall, who as we have seen had been invalided out of the Army,
They had the good fortune to be supported by a competent
staff, some of whom had spent their whole lives in the firm's
service.

The most outstanding, most eccentric and longest lived, was
R. C. Smith, land surveyor. He had been engaged by the first
Alfred at about the time of Edwin's birth, and in 1938 the firm
gave him a gold watch on his completing sixty years' service.

Smith was an austere man, who made it his business to keep the rest of the staff up to the mark. He was a bachelor, a tee-totaller and deeply religious. Once a year he made a pilgrimage on foot from London to Brighton. Arrived at that place of iniquity, he went on the beach and assembled everyone in sight who appeared to have nothing better to do; then he preached them a sermon and prayed fervently for their salvation.

When Smith was approaching 70 the partners agreed it was time to retire him on pension, but were doubtful about how he would react to their proposal. One of them, considered by the others the most tactful, sent for Smith and explained delicately what they had in mind. He explained it so delicately that for several minutes the old man failed to grasp what the interview was about. Suddenly it dawned:

'*Retire? Me retire?* Never heard such nonsense in my life. *Certainly not!*'

With that he stamped out of the room and banged the door. In the event, Smith remained an active member of the staff until he was over 80 and died, as he had wished, in harness.

Another veteran who served during the First World War was Daniels, clerk in charge of the general office. He was deaf and used an ear trumpet; the junior clerks, not wanting to be overheard, used to stuff it with blotting paper. And the dependable Leonard Ives, known to himself and everyone else as 'Mr Alfred's clerk'. There were a number of others, who helped to keep things going in this difficult time, their names may be forgotten, but not their example. Hard-working, unassuming, faithful, they shared the burden.

But no record of the staff of Alfred Savill and Sons would be complete without mention of the remarkable Ambrose Goreham, albeit he belonged to an earlier period and his employment was short-lived.

Goreham, like Smith, had been engaged by Mr Alfred Savill when he was in New Broad Street. If, as is likely, he and Smith were contemporaries, they had little in common. Goreham was intelligent, presentable, and everything the clerk of a distinguished surveyor ought to be. He did his work, when he did it, extremely well. Unhappily it emerged that, when *not* doing it, he was conducting a bookmaker's business for the benefit of the porters in Leadenhall Market on the office premises and in office hours. Mr Savill was vexed. He placed great reliance on Goreham, but there was a limit to what an employer could put up with. He sent for the young man, expressed his displeasure and said it was for Goreham to decide: he could continue as an assistant in a surveyor's office *or* be a bookmaker – but not both.

Goreham opted for the second, and his career as a surveyor ended. But there were no hard feelings and he kept in touch. As a bookmaker, he prospered. Before Alfred Savill died his friend, Ambrose Goreham, owned the Queen's Hotel, Brighton, nearly all of the township of Telscombe east of Brighton, and in 1902 his horse, Shannon Lass, won the Grand National.

But the most valuable member of the staff we have left to the last. In 1917 the firm took an unprecedented step; they brought into partnership the first of a long series of surveyors who were not members of the Savill family. And we must persist in our digression to tell the story of another remarkable man.

George Hubert Eve had been born on 14 March 1879 in the parish of Aveley in South Essex. Like the Savills, he came from an old family of Essex farmers who could trace their lineage back into the seventeenth century, a number of whom in later years became surveyors and valuers. One of the Essex Eves, Richard Eve, born in Hertfordshire in 1788, migrated to Silsoe in Bedfordshire in 1806; there, besides being a farmer, he became a surveyor. He was one of the earliest rating surveyors and in 1825 valued the parish of Silsoe for a fee of fifteen guineas. Richard Eve lived to be 97 and from him are descended the principals in J. R. Eve and Son, and in other distinguished firms of surveyors of that name. The precise relationship between George Eve's ancestors and Richard Eve of Silsoe is uncertain, but there is little doubt that they were of the same stock.

George's grandfather, William Eve, and one of his uncles, William Skinner Eve, who married into the Manning family, were farmers on a large scale. At the turn of the century the Eves and the Mannings were together farming several thousand acres. At about that time Richard Eve, our George Eve's father, left Aveley to take a tenancy of Cranham Hall farm near Upminster. He was a friend of Alfred Savill (Gen. VII, 1829–1905), which accounts for young George's going into that old gentleman's office on leaving school.

At 8 a.m., on the morning of 28 October 1896, George walked down the drive of Cranham Hall to catch the train from Upminster to London and begin his business career. He was dressed in a black morning suit with a starched white shirt and wore a 'topper'. In spite of his impressive appearance they put him in their general office, where he was deemed so unimportant that they paid him nothing for two years. His principal duties were to lick the stamps and post the letters; he subsisted on a cash float of 7s. 6d. a week from his father, over and above the price of his rail ticket. But his father gave him something more valuable than a cash float; it was a piece of advice that George remembered and acted on all his life: 'The only way to get on, my boy, is always to do a little more than the man in the next seat.'

The first Alfred Savill died. Alfred (Gen. VIII, 1854–1928), the eldest of his sons, liked George. They were both so essentially men of the soil; and it is not likely that this second Alfred, who had no son, took a special interest in the boy for that reason? They went on jobs together, George sitting bolt upright in his boss's dog cart. He learned by listening, watching, copying and occasionally asking a trite question. He made himself useful in all sorts of ways, and Alfred came to depend on him. Only one mishap is recorded. Together they attended a farm auction. On arrival George unharnessed the cob and put him out to graze; then, for greater safety, he stacked the bridle, the harness, the carriage lamps, the rug and Alfred's whip in a convenient outbuilding. Alfred was not best pleased at the end of the day, when he discovered that inadvertently the whole lot had been put into the sale!

So George Eve grew up. He developed into a quiet, friendly

man with a twinkle in his eye, whom everyone felt instinctively they could rely on. Inevitably he was promoted in the firm; and, as those from whom he had learned his job grew older, unobtrusively he assumed their duties. Speaking at a Rotary lunch in 1943, he recalled some of his experiences as a surveyor and land agent over fifty years.

One of the first jobs he did alone was on the instruction of Edwin Savill. It was to try to find the title deed of a field called the Vineyard, owned by a client, Mr Henry Long, of Corringham Hall; the field was to be sold in connection with a proposed extension of the Corringham Light Railway. When George got there, Mr Long, a bachelor aged 91, was on his horse in the yard. However, he dismounted and after a prolonged search by the two of them the missing document was found under his bed.

George said that the incident had remained in his memory because the fixing of the boundaries of the new railway was his first contact with that great area of south-east Essex known as Thames-side. When still a comparatively young man, he became involved in a number of important transactions in that part of the county. They concerned among others the Belhus Park estate belonging to the Barrett-Lennard Family; the Coryton estate belonging to Sir Clifford Cory; the Mucking estate belonging to Sir Ebenezer Cox; the West Tilbury estate belonging to the Burness family. He had a keen eye for prospects of development and what today is known by surveyors as 'hope value'; one of his biggest transactions was the purchase for the first Lord Cowdray for development of some 3000 acres between the River Thames and Ockendon railway station.

Eve was a born salesman and a skilful negotiator. He was also one of the leading auctioneers of his time; the following is a story of his first auction.

Mr Alfred Savill was due to hold a sale in the country, but was taken ill at the last moment. He sent a message to George Eve, who normally acted as clerk, and said it was high time Eve became an auctioneer and that he must conduct this sale as a beginning. George was flattered, but more than slightly apprehensive. He was barely 25 and, having no experience, felt he needed a trial run.

Next evening, a few days before the sale, he went into his father's cow shed. The cows, recently milked, fed and watered, were bedded down in their stalls contentedly chewing the cud. George selected three – Daisy, Bluebell, and Rosebud – removed their halters and prodded them to their feet. Then he drove them, bellowing in protest, into a near-by paddock and barred the gate. Grasping a stick to do duty as a hammer, he ascended his rostrum which was a convenient tree stump. The cows, their innate curiosity having overcome their indignation, faced him solemnly as cows do.

'Good evening, ladies, I'm happy to see so many of you here, which is not surprising considering what a desirable property I have to offer. You will have noted from my firm's Particulars that Peaspudding Meadow extends to twelve acres. It's well fenced; there's a spring in the south-west corner; the grass is lush and at the moment full of buttercups. Now who will start me at, say, one hundred and fifty pounds?'

There was silence for a minute, so George put his question again. Then Daisy lifted one of her hind legs in pretence of scratching the underside of her belly.

'Thank you, Madam, I'm very much obliged to you: now which of you ladies will improve on that?'

This time the silence was longer, until George was constrained to take his next bid off a gate-post.

'One hundred and sixty pounds I'm bid! And against you, Miss Daisy – may I say another ten?' Daisy scratched. 'One hundred and seventy pounds I'm bid!'

At that point Bluebell entered the bidding; she was heard to emit a faint moo.

'Thank you indeed, Miss Bluebell, I felt sure you would not let this highly desirable property go for next to nothing. One hundred and eighty pounds I'm bid! What about you, Miss Rosebud?' Rosebud stamped a foot.

'One hundred and ninety pounds I'm now bid! And what about you, Miss Daisy, surely you aren't going to lose it?'

Daisy turned on her heel (or whatever it is a cow turns on) and gave George a sour look. As she walked away she raised her tail disdainfully – *plop . . . plop . . . plop*. Rosebud got it.

Two days later, on 21 September 1905, George Eve took out his first auctioneer's licence. Thereafter he became the firm's sole auctioneer and, so successful was he on the rostrum, he retained that office for more than thirty years.

The war ended, and gradually things returned to normal. Edwin and Norman could give more time to the business and so enable Alfred, their elder brother who was in his sixties, to take life more easily. Eric was demobilized and went to Cambridge to read agriculture. Alfred Cecil, having abandoned his idea of a career in the Regular Army, came into the office and began studying for his professional examinations.

In 1920 the firm moved from Great Winchester Street to 51a Lincoln's Inn Fields, a substantial building in the south-west corner. The decision to leave the City for Holborn was taken after some hesitation; the partners, however, came to the conclusion that their new office was near enough to the City to enable them to maintain their existing contacts, and had the advantage of being among the trustee solicitors who were bringing them new business.

Lydall had now qualified as a chartered surveyor and in 1920 was made a partner. He had married, in 1915, Marjorie Kate Russell, daughter of Colonel Arthur Russell Loscombe, and had by her one son, John Loscombe Lydall Savill (Gen. X, born 27 September 1917), later to be a partner; and a daughter, Suzanne. Lydall preferred the urban to the rural side of the practice, took over the management of the Eyre estate from his father, and went to live in St John's Wood.

Eric, when he had taken his degree, entered the firm's office where he joined Alfred. They both became qualified and were made partners in 1926. Eric had remained a bachelor; Alfred had married, in 1921, Irene Cecilia Dawson, daughter of Cecil Dawson of Brentwood; by her he had one son, Alfred Jonathan M C (Gen. X, born 20 March 1924), and two daughters, Jacqueline and Rosamonde.

Mention must be made at this point of one other young member of the Savill family, who became a partner during this period. Sidney Rowland Savill D S O was a grandson of Ebenezer Savill (Gen. VII, 1835–1911), the brewer; but he had no professional qualifications and the partnership lasted only a short time.

In 1924 Sir Edwin Savill was elected President of the Surveyors' Institution for the ensuing session. He had been a member of council since 1913 and had always taken an active interest in the Institution's affairs.

He delivered his Opening Address in November 1924 and dwelt at some length on the history of the Institution; it had been founded in the year of his birth. He listed the wide variety of subjects chartered surveyors were required to master, divided, as they were at that time, into the Institution's four branches – land agency, valuation, building and quantities, mining. He impressed on the younger members what a mistake it was for a young man, having acquired some knowledge within his branch, to think he could afford to ignore the others. 'Our profession,' he said, 'cannot be put into water-tight compartments – there is continual overlapping.'

Other passages in the Address, directed to the younger members of his audience, are worth quoting:

On asking questions:
Don't be frightened of asking questions, however silly they may turn out to be, and however much they may display your ignorance. Later the time will come when it is advisable to ask sensible questions only – questions which display your knowledge and not your ignorance; but when that time comes your opportunities for picking up odd bits of information are far more limited. Therefore, ask your questions, register the answers firmly in your memory, and don't ask the same question twice.

On guessing:
Guess – on all and every occasion, *guess*. The principal work of a surveyor is to form estimates – at least, as we grow older, we like to call them estimates – and the more we guess when we are young, the better will be our guesses or our estimates when we are older.

On seeing a job through:
Always, if it is in any way possible, see a job through. How often do we see a man who is told to do part of a job, for which he has a special knowledge, hand over his work when he has completed it and never give a thought to the ultimate result? Such a man learns nothing.

On manner and manners (Edwin was not a grandson of Maria Savill for nothing):
I remember when I was young being sent by my father to see a great man in our profession . . . whom I had never seen until I went into his outer office and said: 'Is Mr Jinks in?' At that moment a very tall man came out of an inner room and said: 'What do you want?' I replied: 'I was asking if Mr Jinks was in, Sir.' He looked at me and said: 'Do you always talk to people in their offices with your hat on?' It was a little hard because it was the custom then, as now, not to remove one's hat in the outer office; but it did me good. . . .

The business expanded, Alfred Cecil (the third Alfred), with the consent of his partners, opened a branch office at 7 Birchin Lane in the City of London. Alfred had a flair for finance and thought it a pity that Alfred Savill and Sons, having practised in the City for so long, should have moved out of it. In his judgement the City was the place to make money. He engaged a small staff and brought in to help him one or two promising young men who had the same ideas. Alfred built up a City practice which provided him with an adequate income – but never a fortune. He moved from Birchin Lane to 2 Royal Exchange Buildings, Cornhill, in about 1930. Four years later he moved again – this time to 18 Old Broad Street, where he remained until the outbreak of the Second World War. When Sir Edwin Savill resigned the surveyorship to the Leathersellers in 1937, Alfred was appointed to succeed him.

There was another expansion westward. In 1924 the firm amalgamated with Alexander Turner and Son, who had their head office in North Audley Street and branches in Guildford and Woking. They were mainly estate agents, by which in this context we mean buyers and sellers of houses. It suited the firm thus to broaden the base of its practice and at the same time acquire a West End office. A happy outcome of the merger was that Alexander Wakefield ('Conky') Turner, a lovable man, became a partner in Alfred Savill and Sons, and in 1945 senior partner. He retired in 1965 and lived to a great age.

There were a number of changes in the partnership at about that time. We have seen that Lydall Savill became a partner in 1920 and his brothers, Eric and Alfred, in 1926. Their uncle, the second Alfred, retired in 1921 and went to live in Norfolk where he died in 1928. James George (Jim) Eve was the son of George Hubert Eve who, in his early days, sold Peaspudding Meadow to Rosebud. Jim joined the firm in 1930 on coming down from Cambridge and was made a partner in 1937. So, in the same year, was Peter Laycock, who had served his articles in the office – of whom more in a moment. Finally, in 1938, Frederick Reginald Ragg joined the third Alfred in Old Broad Street. Fred had formerly practised in Birmingham and in Colwyn Bay; his personal clients included the Marquess of Bute, whose family he advised in three successive generations.

Sir Edwin Savill retired in 1937. Something we have not mentioned was his knowledge of wine, on which he was an acknowledged authority. He was very proud of being chairman of the wine committee of the Carlton Club; which leads us to relate the series of happenings that resulted in Peter Laycock, then aged 20, joining his firm.

When Peter left Eton he had expressed an interest in land agency, so arrangements were made for him to go temporarily into the Welbeck estate office to discover what it was about. He found the work interesting and told his father he would like to make it his profession. Now it happened that his father, General Sir Joseph Laycock, was friendly with Colonel Basil Kerr who was agent for the then Duke of Westminster. And it happened that Colonel Kerr mentioned to the general that Sir Edwin Savill was in need of a new assistant. The general immediately wrote to Sir Edwin to ask if he had an opening for his son, whom he described euphemistically as 'a young land agent'; unfortunately he omitted to mention his age or total lack of qualifications. Edwin, impressed, asked Peter to lunch at the Carlton Club, and Peter was happy to accept the invitation.

When they met in the hall Sir Edwin was unable to conceal his astonishment. He said he feared there had been a mistake. He was looking for a qualified assistant with professional experience, besides being considerably older; there was absolutely *no* opening in his office for a boy who had recently left school. Peter was disappointed and probably showed it. Edwin, a kindly man, patted him on the shoulder: 'Never mind; let's go and have lunch.'

He went out of his way to give Peter a good lunch, and towards the end asked him if he liked port. Peter, a little more cheerful by this time, replied that he did. A moment later the bound volume, known in the Carlton Club as the 'wine list', was placed on the table before Edwin. He put on his spectacles, opened the volume at the page headed 'Port', and went slowly down the list of vintages with his thumb. He beckoned the waiter, told him the bin number and ordered a half-bottle. Then he handed back the wine list; but not before Peter, who had good eyesight, had noted where his thumb had stopped – Croft 1912.

Presently the waiter came back with the wine in a decanter, and Edwin broke off the conversation to taste it. He nodded his approval and their glasses were filled.

'This, my boy, is a vintage port and I hope you'll like it. I don't suppose it would mean anything were I to tell you the name of the shipper?'

The temptation was as instant and irresistible as many of those temptations we mortals yield to.

'No, Sir, probably not.' Peter sipped the wine. Then, diffidently, he added: 'I suppose, Sir, it's not by chance a Croft?'

Sir Edwin positively jumped in his chair. It was the second time he had been astonished that afternoon:

'Good God, boy, you're right; it *is* a Croft! You must have a natural palate. Now tell me, what year?'

Peter, committed, thought it wise to go cautiously and deliberately misjudged the date: 'Possibly the 1908?'

'Amazing!' exclaimed his host, '*amazing* – only four years out!' Then he drained his glass, leaned back in his chair and was silent for at least three minutes. It seemed an age to Peter, fearful lest the truth should dawn. At last he spoke – and it hadn't.

'I've been thinking about the office and we'll take you on. Your salary will be a hundred pounds a year and you'll be articled to my brother, Norman. He will charge a hundred and fifty pounds a year. Take one from the other and it leaves fifty; your father will pay that.'

Thus it was that Peter Laycock, by virtue of a half-bottle of vintage port, came to enter the office of Alfred Savill and Sons where he remained for more than forty years.

At about the time of Peter's arrival, Edwin's second son, Eric Savill, took his departure. His partners were sad, but his resignation was understandable. Eric was an agriculturist, and since joining the firm ten years earlier had been concerned mainly with its country managements. At that time they were all conducted from London, and the atmosphere of the busy office in Lincoln's Inn Fields had never appealed to him.

He had received a letter from the Commissioner of Crown Lands inquiring whether he would be interested in the post of Deputy Surveyor of Windsor Parks and Woods. Eric said later: 'I hated London, where I was then living, and thought it was the sort of job that might suit me.' He accepted. Six years afterwards, at the suggestion of the Ranger who was King George VI, he was promoted Deputy Ranger and held that office until his retirement in 1959.

The royal estate includes lands at Windsor, Virginia Water, Ascot, Swinley and Bagshot. The Great Park stretches from Windsor in the north to Sunninghill in the south, and is bounded on the west by Windsor Forest. In the reign of George II (1727–1760) it was part of a great expanse of wasteland, interspersed by clearings where humble people lived – very similar, one imagines, to Epping Forest during the same period. Then William, Duke of Cumberland, was appointed Ranger and His Royal Highness had a taste for lakes. Virginia Water, Obelisk Pond, Johnson's Pond and Great Meadow Pond were devised in his time. George III ('Farmer George'), more interested in the countryside than his father, ordered big areas to be cleared, drained and cultivated. The process of reclamation was continued under successive monarchs until the whole of the Park, some 4500 acres, became the splendid tract of country it is now.

During the Second World War, as had happened during the First, much of the Great Park was ploughed up and farmed. King George VI insisted that every acre suitable for the production of foodstuffs should be used for that purpose. That was the responsibility of the Deputy Ranger. Foodstuffs from the royal farms included milk, and Eric Savill built up one of the finest herds of pedigree Friesians in the United Kingdom based on the Terling herd belonging to Lord Rayleigh.

Eric was fortunate in his home. Ranger's Lodge, in the Great Park, is a delightful house and his mother Lady (Helen) Savill had come to share it. He inherited her gift for landscape gardening and had not been slow in putting it to use. In 1932, with the approval of King George V and Queen Mary, he had embarked on what was to become the paramount interest of his life. At that time there was no royal garden at Windsor except that at Frogmore, the East Terrace beside the Castle designed by Wyattville for George IV, and formal gardens under its walls. Eric's plan was to find a suitable site in the Great Park and there establish a different sort of garden; he had in mind a setting of fine old trees, broad vistas, winding paths, grassy swards, ponds and streams, banks of flowering shrubs and shy retreats for woodland plants.

Such a site was found. It was heavily overgrown, but its lie was pleasantly undulating; ponds at different levels had been linked by a stream, now no more than a ditch. The soil was what Eric wanted – an acid loam. There were ancient oaks in what once had been water meadows, a beech wood, sweet chestnuts and silver birch. And to the west, bordering the plain known as Smith's Lawn, a windbreak of firs.

The first step was to dig out the upper pond in the north-west corner; it had silted up. Then to enlarge the lower pond and bring the stream, so long captive, back to life. It gurgled once more and tumbled gaily over boulders into deep, green pools. Thereafter to plant the banks – with primulas of many kinds, ferns in abundance, iris, meadowsweet and golden kingcups –

> Where oxlips and the nodding violet grows
> Quite over-canopied by luscious woodbine
> With sweet musk roses, and with eglantine.

The major task that first winter was clearance – a major task indeed! Great masses of tangled undergrowth were uprooted and burned. Trees intended for preservation were clearly marked and all the others cut down. Then, bit by bit over the years, the rest of the garden was made and planted. Rhododendrons in wide variety, azaleas, magnolias, camellias, hydrangeas, lilies; roses in profusion – shrub roses, floribunda roses; grass rides and herbaceous borders; a massive wall of mellowed brick mantled with rock plants; an Alpine meadow . . . and so we could go on.

The woodland garden was not the only royal garden made by Eric Savill in Windsor Great Park; he was soon to begin on the valley garden near Virginia Water, which is complementary. But the woodland garden was the first and quickly became famous; today, people from all over the world, including learned horticulturists, go to Windsor to see it.

Sir Eric Savill, as he had become, retired as Deputy Ranger in 1959. He remained, however, Director of the Royal Gardens at the express wish of Her Majesty Queen Elizabeth II. His mother had died in 1956 and he retired finally in 1970 to a charming house, built for him by the Commissioners and approved personally by the Queen, near his beloved gardens and overlooking Smith's Lawn.

Eric was fortunate in many things, most of all in the encouragement he received from his patrons. So many of the Royal Family are, or have been, enthusiastic gardeners. One of his first jobs after appointment was to advise the Prince of Wales, later King Edward VIII, on the replanning of his garden at Fort Belvedere. And when the Duke and Duchess of York (as they then were) were busy with their garden at Royal Lodge, Eric, a mile away, was busy with his. They compared notes and went to admire each other's roses; so began a friendship between the two men that lasted until the King's death. Eric was made MVO in 1938, CBE in 1946, CVO in 1951 and KCVO in 1955. But a further honour, bestowed on him by King George VI in 1951, may be deemed the highest. By royal command the woodland garden, his creation, was named 'The Savill Garden' for all time.

And so we end our chapter amid the glory of that garden. For Eric Savill, its designer, may the ending of the chapter be long deferred. One day they will say of him, as of an earlier architect: 'If you require a monument, look around.'

8

Between the wars

Norman Savill and his country managements – royalty disillusioned – the Wimborne estates – Viscount Wimborne and the Ritz Hotel – rates, rating and ratepayers – town and country planning – depression in the nineteenthirties – royal abdication – gathering clouds again – Corporal Hitler – meeting at Munich

Norman Savill (Gen. VIII) was more than five years younger than Edwin Savill and twenty years younger than their elder brother, Alfred. Although his father took him into partnership before he died in 1905, Norman had been a late starter in the firm. He was educated at Harrow, where he was in the same house as Winston Churchill who was eight months younger. On leaving Harrow his father had put him into the office of Price Waterhouse and Company with a view to his becoming a chartered accountant; in Alfred's judgement his own business was not large enough to afford a living for more than two of his sons. But later he changed his mind, took Norman away from Price Waterhouse and insisted on his joining the other two. Norman, who had qualified as an accountant, resented this change of plan; but what their father said was law and there was nothing to be gained by arguing. In the event, the dual qualification of chartered accountant and chartered surveyor must have stood him in good stead and been appreciated by the owners of the estates he looked after; and it was always accepted that the financial aspect of the partnership was in Norman's department.

He was not interested in the urban side of the practice and more than content to leave that to Edwin; nor was he interested in the agricultural valuations and farm sales undertaken by his eldest brother, Alfred, and latterly by George Eve. What Norman enjoyed were personal appointments as agent for individual landowners. He had inherited from his father some of the agencies we mentioned earlier – Bishops Hall for Lord Lambourne, Loughton Hall for the Maitlands, Mark Hall for the Arkwrights, and others. As time went by he acquired new agencies of his own, although some of the most important did not come until he was in middle age. He became agent for Wyndham Radclyffe, a Cardiff shipowner, whose estate in Glamorgan ran to some 10000 acres; for Sir Pierce Lacey at Ampton near Bury St Edmunds; for Lord Stradbroke in Suffolk; and he managed for a time the Dean Park estate in Northamptonshire belonging to the Brudenells.

Shortly before the outbreak of the Second World War Norman bought the Barnwell estate, near Oundle, for the Duke of Gloucester. The intention had been for the agent for the Duke of Buccleuch, who was the Duke of Gloucester's father-in-law, to manage it. But war came and Norman Savill looked after the property for several years until his successor was available to take over. One day the Duke of Gloucester made it known that he and the Duchess would like to make a little tour of the estate and meet some of the tenant farmers. Norman made the necessary arrangements, and when the day arrived was accompanied by his clerk, a Yorkshireman called Featherstone, who was not renowned for tact.

On leaving one of the farm houses, where the Duke and Duchess had been treated with respect bordering on reverence, the Duke asked Norman if he had noticed a framed portrait of himself and the Duchess in a place of honour in the parlour. He was obviously touched and said he wondered how long it had hung there. Norman was about to reply, but Featherstone got in first: 'Five minutes, I'd guess, your Royal Highness!'

In 1933 Norman Savill succeeded to the management of the Canford estate, near Wimborne in Dorset, the property of Viscount Wimborne. It was probably the firm's biggest management at that time and led to the opening of the Wimborne office which has always been one of the busiest of the country offices.

Lord Wimborne's family, like the Savills, had once been yeomen farmers. Over the years, by dint of imagination, application and hard work, they had become internationally famous.

John Guest, farmer, was born at Broseley in Shropshire in 1722. He interested himself in coal-mining and iron smelting, and in 1763, with a partner named Wilkinson, leased a property on the River Taff in Glamorgan from the Earl of Plymouth. He soon became manager of the nearby Merthyr Furnace, which was the nucleus of what eventually became the great Dowlais Ironworks. His son, Josiah John Guest, was appointed manager of the Dowlais Iron Company and by 1851 was in sole control of it.

The company prospered exceedingly as coal-miners and iron-masters. Their pig-iron was processed into tramroad rails and later into railroad rails, and they supplied a number of the new railway companies including the line from Stockton to Darlington which opened in 1821. Among their customers were the Navy Board, the East India Company, and the governments of the United States, France, Russia, the Netherlands, Portugal, Egypt and China.

In 1833 Josiah John Guest had married Lady Charlotte Bertie, daughter of the ninth Earl of Lindsey, and when he died in 1852 the family business, which is known today as GKN (Guest, Keen and Nettlefold), was left in trust for their children. He had been made a baronet in 1838 and his eldest son, Ivor Bertie Guest, was created the first Baron Wimborne. Ivor Churchill Guest, eldest son of Baron Wimborne, became the first Viscount. The present head of the family is the third Viscount.

The Canford estate, in south-east Dorset, was purchased by Sir Josiah Guest from Lord de Mauley, a son of the Earl of Bessborough, in 1846, for £335000. It then extended to 11280 acres. Parts have since been sold including some of the larger farms, and land near Poole and Bournemouth for development.

For nearly a hundred years the estate had been looked after by resident agents. When the last of these died in 1933, the first Viscount appointed Norman Savill as agent for Canford, also for a family estate at Ashby St Ledgers in Northamptonshire; Norman managed Canford from the office in Parkstone that had been used by his predecessors. When, as we shall see presently, he died in 1945, the management of both estates was entrusted to Alfred Savill and Sons and their office in Wimborne dates from then.

An agreeable story is told of the first Viscount Wimborne, who had a dry sense of humour. His London residence was Wimborne House, a mansion on the west side of Arlington Street, St James's, now occupied by the Eagle Star Insurance Company. It has a pleasant garden, backing on the Green Park, and adjoining it on the north at the corner of Piccadilly is the Ritz Hotel.

One morning Lord Wimborne received a letter from the managing director of the Ritz Hotel Company. He presented his compliments and ventured to inquire, very respectfully, whether his lordship would consider selling the company a small part of his property to enable the hotel to enlarge its kitchen. His lordship replied, very courteously, in the negative. He added: 'What a remarkable coincidence! I was about to write to ask whether your company would kindly sell me a small part of its hotel to enable me to enlarge my dining room.'

We recorded earlier that Norman Savill had married in 1900 Jane, daughter of Charles Crofton Black of Buckhurst Hill. That marriage was dissolved and he married again in 1928. By his second wife, Jean, daughter of Edward Gill of Birmingham, he had one son, Henry Edward Savill (Gen. IX, b. 1929) who is today a partner in the firm.

All Norman Savill's managements during the interwar period – indeed, all the firm's managements – were affected more or less by a spate of legislation. Surveyors and land agents throughout the country were kept busy, first in mastering and thereafter in applying it; they were beset with anxieties lest by inadvertence they should miss some statutory 'appointed day' and involve a client in loss. Among the subjects of this legislation two were far-reaching; the first was rates and rating, and the second town and country planning.

'Rates', the name we give to taxes levied for the purposes of local government in respect of the occupation of land, are not so ancient as tithe, but their origin is nearly four centuries back in our history. The modern 'general rate', to meet the annual cost of a variety of public services, is a lineal descendant of the 'poor rate' under the Poor Relief Act 1601, commonly called the 'Statute of Elizabeth I'.

Under that Act the 'overseers', who were parishioners, were required to 'set the poor to work'; also

to raise weekly by taxation of every inhabitant parson vicar and other, and of every occupier of lands, houses, tithes, impropriate or propriations of tithes, coal mines or saleable underwoods, in the said parish in such competent sums of money as they shall think fit . . . for and towards the necessary relief of the lame impotent old blind and such other among them being poor and not able to work, and also for the putting out of such children to be apprentices, to be gathered out of the same parish, according to the ability of the same parish.

Today the 'competent sum of money' required of an inhabitant is the amount he pays in rates, generally half-yearly, based on the assessment of the 'hereditament' he occupies. The assessment is a reflection of its rental value. Broadly, the rateable value is the rent at which it might reasonably be expected to let from year to year after deducting a statutory allowance for the annual cost of maintenance. Should a ratepayer improve his property, its assessment will go up; and we have noted how Henry George and other economists inveighed against a system whereby a person, who creates wealth for the ultimate benefit of the community by his efforts, is taxed for having done so. The explanation is that in the time of Elizabeth I there was no income tax and no means of assessing the amount of a person's income. It was generally accepted as being just that he should contribute to the relief of the poor according to his means, and the value of the house he occupied was the only available yardstick.

The modern rating authority are successors to the Elizabethan overseers. They have a duty to collect the rates and are also a spending authority; in the 1920s they were also responsible for making and revising the assessments. But there were inconsistencies in the level of the assessments between one area and another, and the Rating and Valuation Act of 1925 was designed to correct them. The whole of England and Wales was to be revalued by or on behalf of the rating authorities, and there were to be quinquennial valuations to keep the valuation lists up to date.*

The revaluation under the 1925 Act was scarcely complete before further nation-wide valuations were required under the Rating and Valuation (Apportionment) Act of 1928. The intention of the government was to 'derate' agricultural land and buildings (i.e. relieve them from all rates), and partially to derate certain other classes of property known as 'industrial' and 'freight-transport' hereditaments. That was accomplished by the Local Government Act 1931. The purpose of the 1928 Act was to provide machinery for splitting the total assessments of industrial and freight-transport hereditaments between the rateable portions and non-rateable portions.

Alfred Savill and Sons were not specialist rating surveyors, geared to valuing large areas for rating authorities. The firm of J. R. Eve and Son, by contrast, undertook the revaluation of the entire county of Bedford. Inevitably, however, the Savills had to satisfy themselves as to the fairness of the new assessments on the estates they managed, besides acting for clients who were 'aggrieved' by what they deemed excessive increases or unfair apportionments. For that purpose they entered into an arrangement with a singular young man called John A. F. Watson. He had been articled to an old firm of chartered surveyors in St James's and had lately been employed by J. R. Eve and Son in connection with their valuation of Bedfordshire. Having joined

*Since 1948 the responsibility for making and amending rating assessments has belonged to the valuation officers of the Inland Revenue.

a firm called Ferris and Puckridge in the City of London, he was trying to build up a rating practice. The arrangement, which suited both parties, was for Alfred Savill and Sons to pass their rating work to John Watson on a fee-sharing basis. This was John Watson's first contact with the firm in which he was destined, years afterwards, to become a partner.

Town and country planning, as we know it today, derives basically from the Town and Country Planning Act 1932. There had been earlier measures. The first was the Housing Act 1909, which empowered local authorities to make planning schemes 'as respects any land which is in course of development or appears likely to be used for building purposes with the general object of securing proper sanitary conditions, amenity and convenience in connection with the laying out and user of the lands and of any neighbouring lands'.

These early planning powers had been widened by an Act of 1919, which obliged local authorities with a population of 20 000 and upward to submit schemes for approval by the Local Government Board within a specified period. Further powers were conferred by Acts of 1923 and 1925, and by the Local Government Act of 1929 to which we have referred.

The Town and Country Planning Act 1932 repealed nearly all this legislation. Hitherto the powers of the local authorities had been confined to land not yet built on; the 1932 Act extended their powers to all land, built on or not, including land unlikely to be developed at all. The Local Government Board were replaced by the Minister of Health; and the Minister was made responsible for approving all planning schemes, which then became binding on the parties. Compensation was payable to anyone who had suffered injury as the result of a scheme coming into operation; conversely, the planning authority became entitled to 75 per cent of any increase in value ('betterment') that had accrued to the landowner. In the event, few planning schemes made under the provisions of the 1932 Act ever came into operation – so entitlement to compensation or liability to pay betterment seldom arose. But this was the first attempt, under planning law, to equate what is sometimes called *comp* to the will-o'-the-wisp called *bett*.

The third decade of the twentieth century was restless and fraught with anxieties. The first Labour government in 1924, under Ramsay Macdonald, had been short-lived. The Conservative government under Stanley Baldwin, which followed it, lasted until 1929. Then Macdonald came back, this time with Liberal support. But the new government soon ran into financial difficulties, and during the 'great depression' of the early thirties unemployment reached an unprecedented level. In July 1931 a report by the Economy Committee, under the chairmanship of Lord May, predicted worse to come; the sequel was a flight from the pound by foreign investors and heavy falls in our gold reserves.

Ramsay Macdonald's efforts to contain the situation were frustrated by his left-wing colleagues, who declined to support his prosposed cuts in expenditure. So in July he went to the King and told him he was unable to continue. The King called a conference, which Stanley Baldwin (Conservative) and Herbert Samuel (Liberal) were invited to attend. The outcome was the first all-party coalition ('national') government under Macdonald, at whom some of his former associates yelled 'Traitor!' At another general election in March 1932 the coalition gained all but fifty-seven seats in the Commons and he remained in office until June 1935. There followed a succession of coalition governments until the end of the Second World War – under Baldwin (June 1935–May 1937), Neville Chamberlain (May 1937–May 1940), Winston Churchill (May 1940–May 1945).

King George V died on 20 January 1936; his son, King Edward VIII, was never crowned. The fact of the new king's attachment to Mrs Simpson, who had been through the divorce court, was first denied in high places and then swept surreptitiously under the royal carpet. It was common knowledge by the autumn. The lady was unacceptable as queen, and a tentative suggestion for a morganatic marriage was firmly turned down by the Dominion governments. As the King was adamant, abdication appeared the only way out. And abdication, predicted gloomy old gentlemen in West End clubs, would be 'the end of everything'. He abdicated in December, and it wasn't.

Abroad were wars and rumours of wars. For ten years after the Versailles Treaty in 1919 a certain complacency had been discernible in Europe. The 'war to end wars' was over; the Allies had won it; thank God for that. Britain, France and other allied nations showed a tendency to try to restore the prewar order; there was a general agreement on the need to create and maintain an international monetary system based on the gold standard. In the meantime the League of Nations was acting as a kind of super-policeman. But by the end of 1933, after the worldwide economic crisis of the preceding years, there had been a general abandonment of the gold standard; and the League of Nations, having failed to prevent the Greek invasion of Turkey in 1921, was to be equally ineffective in preventing the Italian invasion of Abyssinia in 1935, and the Japanese invasion of the Chinese Republic in 1937.

In Germany there was no such complacency. A proud nation had been conquered and humiliated. She had been shorn of her provinces. The Rhineland was occupied by her conquerers. Her armies had been disbanded, her fleet sunk, and the smallest air force was proscribed. Her unpaid bill for reparations was enormous, if more than offset ('Curiouser and curiouser!' cried Alice) by totally unsecured loans from America and Great Britain. Then, in the economic crisis, financial aid suddenly dried up; factories had to be closed and imaginative enterprises, on whose prosperity the new Germany so largely depended, were ruined. During the winter of 1930 her unemployment topped $2\frac{1}{2}$ millions. The government of the Weimar republic, which the Germans regarded as an imposition by the enemy, could no longer cope. 'Thereafter mighty forces were adrift, the void was open, and into that void after a pause there strode a maniac of ferocious genius, the repository and expression of the most virulent hatreds that have ever corroded the human breast – Corporal Hitler.'*

*Winston S. Churchill, *The Second World War*, vol. 1, 1948.

The National Socialist (Nazi) Party came into office for the first time in February 1933. The ageing Hindenburg, President of the Reich, appointed Adolf Hitler as Chancellor. Gradually but inexorably Hitler gained power until, on Hindenburg's death in August 1934, he assumed the title 'Führer' and became the effective dictator of Germany.

Hitler had wasted no time while Chancellor. His enemies and rivals had been rounded up and murdered on the 'night of the long knives' (30 June 1934). He had launched a campaign of wholesale extermination against the Jews, for whom he nursed an obsessional hatred. There followed a series of aggressions in open defiance of the Versailles treaty. Germany was rearming. In 1935 she reoccupied the Rhineland. In 1938 she announced her intention to annex Austria and the Sudeten portion of Czechoslovakia. Eventually the British Conservative government, under Neville Chamberlain, thought it time to call a halt and Hitler was warned that if he persisted in his avowed intention it would mean war. In September war was imminent; the fleet was mobilized and air-raid shelters were being dug in Hyde Park. At the very last moment Chamberlain accepted an invitation from Hitler to fly out and see him personally. The Munich agreement followed and provided among other things for the virtual dismemberment of Czechoslovakia. But Chamberlain on his return was elated. He proclaimed: 'I believe it is peace for our time.'

The Prime Minister was deceived. At the Nuremburg trials it was conceded that Hitler's sole purpose in signing the agreement had been to give Germany more time to rearm. She had then continued doing so. So did we, aware at long last of the deplorable weakness of our national defences due to the blindness and procrastination of politicians. It is open to question whether Germany or the Allies gained more from the breathing space.

In January 1939 Ribbentrop, Hitler's Foreign Minister, opened a diplomatic offensive against Poland. Germany had territorial ambitions on the Baltic, and should she achieve them Poland would be encircled. The Polish government strongly resisted the German proposals, which were not long in becoming threats.

Chamberlain was disillusioned and aghast. In March 1939 Great
Britain and France jointly guaranteed Poland's frontiers. Hitler
appeared undeterred and it was a summer of nerve-racking
suspense. On 1 September he invaded Poland; Great Britain and
France mobilized forthwith; on 3 September 1939, for the second
time in twenty-five years, Great Britain and Germany were at
war.

9

1939–45: Hitler's war

'Dig for victory' – Munich breathing space – stimulus for agriculture – evacuation and dispersal – requisitioning and was damage, how the owners were compensated this time – doodle bugs and rockets – Lydall's death (1940) – Peter Laycock (b. 1910) Alfred Cecil's death (1943) – 'All wars are the same' – the inept angler

Most of what happened at home in the Second World War was a repetition, but more intense, of the happenings in the First. Air raids were on a vastly greater scale and the black-out was enforced more rigorously. The official scheme for evacuation was something new. We were better off for food, although most of it was rationed. Clothing was rationed, which it had not been previously. A shortage of petrol hit harder because more people owned cars. There were more slogans: 'Dig for victory!' 'Lend to defend the right to be free!' 'Give us the tools and we'll finish the job!' 'Is your journey really necessary?' 'Walls have ears – be like Dad, keep Mum!'

In the Second World War, understandably, we were more fearful of invasion. The Home Guard built concrete pill boxes at remote country cross-roads and sometimes, for no apparent strategic reason, in the middle of big fields. Enemy parachutists must be outwitted, so we uprooted all the sign posts and painted out the name boards on all railway stations. A German agent, ordered to report on the railway system from Dover to Penzance, warned his masters: 'Curiously, all the places on the main line bear the same name – "GENTLEMEN".' In short, we had learned from experience how to conduct a war on the home front. On the whole we made a better job than on the last occasion and the post-Munich breathing space was helpful in connection with more things than those we have mentioned.

We have recorded the splendid response by British farmers to the urgent demand for higher food production during the latter part of the First World War. They may well have been embittered by what befell them afterwards. The Corn Production Act 1917 with its minimum price for cereals was a temporary measure, and when it expired in 1922 the guarantees lapsed. In the meantime, a regrettable consequence of Great Britain, the United States and Japan restoring the former value of their currencies, all the agricultural nations experienced a spectacular fall in prices. In this country they fell by nearly half, and the capital of the farmers had to be written down accordingly. Many sought a living in other spheres and a number went bankrupt. There was no money for fertilizers or improvements, and the derating of agricultural land in 1931 was the merest palliative. Thousands of acres of arable land that had yielded good harvests in wartime tumbled down to bad grass.

In 1937, the year before Munich, the Chamberlain government had at last awakened to what was happening, and the possibility of another war impelled action. A new farming and ploughing–up policy was devised and the breathing space, short as it was, afforded a chance to develop it. Subsidies were again made available and agricultural executive committees were again appointed. War came, and the early years saw the recruitment of the Women's Land Army. Cereal crops were increased by 80 per cent and the potato acreage doubled; the ley system, long established in Scotland, was introduced south of the Border. Agriculture was again thriving. It is a melancholy reflection that it took two world wars, independent of each other, to revive an industry that had been allowed to stagnate and achieve the production of which it was capable.

One of the advantages we gained from the breathing space was an opportunity to implement the recommendations of the Committee on Evacuation which had reported in July 1938. It was recognized that in any future war air invasion was to be expected on a much greater scale than in the 1914–18 war. Non-essential persons, including children, would need to be moved out of the target areas. The committee said: 'The whole issue . . . may well turn on the manner in which the problem of evacuation from densely populated areas is handled.'

They recommended that all schemes for evacuation should be voluntary unless a district had been rendered uninhabitable. The main-line railways were to be the principal means of transport. Refugees on arriving in the reception areas were to be billeted in private households, and the local authorities must make surveys to assess the amount of potential accommodation. 'Plans should be made in complete detail for the transference of children of school age, school by school, to places of greater safety.'

The government had planned accordingly. Readers of the older generation will remember, when war came, the long queues of school children, each child with its gas mask in a cardboard box hanging round its neck, on the platforms and in the fore-courts of the railway stations. Mothers with young children, if willing to leave their husbands, travelled independently. At the other end billeting officers, recruited by the local authority, were waiting on the station platforms; among them were the wives and daughters of large and small landowners and the staffs of local estate offices. So it was that the town went to the country, and for the first time one half of the world saw how the other half lived. Neither was impressed.

But for months there was no bombing. What the government had failed to anticipate was that many parents, lulled into a false sense of security, would bring their children home again. The spring of 1940 was the beginning of the blitz, and in nearly every vulnerable area, to a greater or less extent, evacuation had to be a repeat performance. A constant trafficking to and fro between the evacuation and reception areas, according to the current intensity of enemy action, was to become a major administrative problem.

But it was not only women, children and retired people who

were evacuated. Many private firms, manufacturers and not a few government departments had arranged to move their head-quarters into relatively safe areas, where they hoped to carry on their work undisturbed. Alfred Savill and Sons were among them. Shortly after Munich, Norman Savill, head of the firm since Edwin's retirement the previous year, called the staff together and expounded the plan he and his partners had made.

Should there be war, Peter Laycock, who held a commission in the Territorial Army, would be called up at once; also, no doubt, junior members of the staff. It was also possible that the firm would lose Alfred Savill, who, although in his forties, was on the Regular Reserve of Officers. The remaining partners, in order of seniority, were Norman Savill, Lydall Savill, George Eve, Conky Turner, Jim Eve and Fred Ragg.

The policy was to disperse. Norman Savill, with vital records and the cash office, was to go to the Parkstone (later Wimborne) office in Dorset. The architects, under F. W. Charity, were to go to the Woking office. Featherstone and a secretary were bound for the Wimborne estate office at Ashby St Ledgers. Should Alfred go, the City office would be closed. The partners, other than Norman, were to remain centred on Lincoln's Inn Fields with a skeleton staff.

When war broke out the plan was put into effect. A year later Norman Savill and a senior member of the staff, Charles Shores, joined others of Lord Wimborne's advisers in Malmesbury; for the rest of the war the management of all the Wimborne estates was conducted from there.

As during the First World War, much of the firm's work in all its offices was in relation to the requisitioning of land and buildings. The compensation (Defence) Act 1939 (Royal Assent, 1 September 1939) had laid down the basis of compensation payable to landowners for land taken. In brief, it was to be the annual rental value under a lease, assumed to have been granted immediately before the beginning of 'the emergency', the lessee paying rates and taxes and bearing the cost of maintenance.

Compensation was thus pegged at 1939 values. That basis was to remain throughout the war, subject to percentage supplements under later instruments.

During the 'phoney war', before the bombing began, there was time to put the finishing touches to the schemes for compensation for war damage that had been devised during the Munich breathing space. A commission, entitled the War Damage Commission, was to administer the schemes. The War Damage Act of 1943, which consolidated two previous Acts, contained 128 sections and 8 schedules. Payments were to be made 'out of monies provided by Parliament', in respect of damage to land (and buildings) during the 'risk period'. The Board of Trade were to operate schemes for the insurance of goods. Part I of the Act was concerned with land and buildings; Part II with goods; Part III was miscellaneous.

Contributions to meet the cost of payments under Part I were universal and compulsory, to be apportioned among landlords, tenants and mortgagees. There were to be two main classes of payment. The first was a 'cost of works payment', the second a 'value payment'.

A cost of works payment was the actual cost of making good the damage if that was an economic proposition. A value payment was the amount of the depreciation in the value of the property if it was uneconomic, and applied only when it had been totally destroyed or was irreparable; and in computing a value payment 'the value of a hereditament in any state shall be ascertained by reference to prices current at 31 March 1939'. 1939 level of values again.

Part II of the Act provided two schemes for the insurance of goods. The 'business scheme' was compulsory; the Board of Trade undertook to insure goods belonging to someone for the purpose of his business. Under the 'private chattels scheme' the Board undertook to insure goods owned privately.

But the assessment of compensation for property that had been requisitioned or suffered war damage was only part of the manifold responsibilities shouldered by surveyors and land agents.

New problems arose in connection with estate management. For example, a lessee was permitted in certain circumstances summarily to 'disclaim' his lease. Determinations of compensation and the exercise by tenants of their statutory rights were appealable, and firms like Alfred Savill and Sons were kept busy. Again and again their clients' London estates were damaged. Houses deemed capable of repair had to be shored up, others pulled down. Bombed-out tenants had to be rehoused. Families, returning unexpectedly from the reception areas to find their homes in ruins, had to be coped with. The blitz was at its height between May 1940 and the end of 1941. During the next two-and-a-half-years air attacks on London and other great cities were intermittent, though sometimes devastating.

In June 1944 Londoners had their first taste of the pilotless plane called by its German inventors the V1, but nicknamed by us the 'fly bomb', the 'buzz bomb' or the 'doodle bug'. It was followed in September by the V2, a giant rocket with a war-head of about the same size as that of the V1. Unlike the V1, which arrived noisily and allowed people time to lie on their faces or take cover, the V2 came silently, which explains why on average the V2 caused proportionately twice as many casualties. The figures for London are revealing. About 2,400 V1s reached their target and the civilian casualties were 6,184 killed and 17,987 gravely injured. Only about 500 V2s descended on London and the totals of civilians killed and injured were 2,724 and 6,476 respectively.

Jim Eve, the junior partner, was an agriculturist and his was a 'reserved occupation'. We had learned our lesson in the First War, and on this occasion we were not going to conscript into the armed forces the specialists upon whom we would have to rely for producing our food. Jim and his father, with a depleted staff, had to cope with the many and diverse problems that arose under war conditions on agricultural estates under the firm's management all over the country. Jim Eve was also a member of the estates subcommittee of the Essex War Agricultural Executive Committee and of the Home Guard.

Lydall Savill died after a short illness in 1940. His first marriage to Marjorie Loscombe, by whom he had one son, John Loscombe Lydall Savill, and one daughter, had been dissolved. He had married secondly Margaret, daughter of William Huxtable Thorne, a judge of the Supreme Court of the Straits Settlements; by her he had another son, Timothy Lydall Savill, born in 1940, and another daughter. Lydall's death at such a time was a grievous loss to the firm, but more grievous to his friends. It is no reflection on the Savill family to say he was not a typical Savill. There was nothing forceful or even brusque about him and even when he felt strongly he was seldom first to express an opinion; it was his nature to be tolerant of the views of others. Lydall was a sensitive man, possibly shy, whose outstanding quality was his gentleness. Maria, his forbear, whose maiden name he bore, would have loved him; no matter whom he met or dealt with, 'the courtesy would be the same'.

Peter Laycock, as had been expected, was called up at the outbreak. He was a captain in the Notts. Sherwood Rangers Yeomanry (Cavalry), and they embarked for Palestine with their horses in January 1940; later they trained as field gunners. Thence to North Africa, where he took part in Wavell's offensive as far as Benghazi and back again to Tobruk. From 1941 to 1942 he was ADC to Oliver Lyttleton (as he then was), Minister of State, who was temporarily stationed in Cairo. Peter returned to England, was promoted major and became second-in-command of No. 10 (International) Commando which consisted of six troops of six different nationalities. Two years later, now lieutenant-colonel, he commanded No. 10 and saw further active service in the Netherlands. Peter Laycock's decorations include Knight Officer Orange Nassau with Swords (Holland); l'Ordre de la Couronne avec Palme, and Croix de Guerre avec Palme (both Belgium); and King Haakon VII of Norway's Liberty Cross.

Another partner who achieved a fine record of military service in the Second World War was some thirteen years older. Alfred Savill (Gen. IX, b. 1897) was the youngest of Sir Edwin's three sons. The reader will recall that in 1914, at the outbreak of war, he had been intended for a career in the Regular Army, that he was commissioned in the Royal Field Artillery at the age of 17, served in France from 1914 to 1918, was gassed and wounded, awarded the Military Cross and Bar, and retired to the Regular Army Reserve of Officers when the war ended.

But his health had suffered and he was granted a permanent 40 per cent disability pension. The staff were surprised when 'Major Alfred' was recalled in July 1939 and passed fit for further service. He was commissioned in the 30th Field Regiment RA and crossed to France in September. Later he was transferred to the 56th Anti-Tank Regiment and given command of a battery.

Little happened for eight months. He told his wife he was 'frantically busy'; but Alfred was a man of immense energy and it is evident from some of the letters he wrote her that he was finding the waiting period tedious:

On war:
All wars are alike – endless delays alternating with feverish activity.

On returning from leave:
Back again to the old boredom.

About the enemy, after inspecting an infantry advance post:
There's a sort of tacit understanding that if they'll refrain from potting us we'll do likewise . . . It's really all too ludicrous.

About staff officers at headquarters:
Such a queer lot of 'no account' people – petty, fussy, stupid and appalling sticklers for complying with the written word . . . How relieved I shall be when the British Army is engaged in active operations and no longer has time to engage in these aggravating trivialities

He had not long to wait. From a letter, written hastily in pencil, headed 'BEF, 21 May':

Darling, this is just too horrifyingly awful for words and I'm not going to attempt to describe the last ten days, and all I want to do is to shut the whole thing out of my mind. They got across [the river] this morning and we've been counter-attacking all day and by the look of it we shall re-establish the position by nightfall. So far my battery is still intact, but we've had the hell of a time and the men are badly shaken and just about all in. I don't mind confessing to anyone that I'm a bit shaken myself. It's much worse than anything I went through in the last war. So many more attacks from aeroplanes. Tanks etc. and everything moving at such an appalling pace and the shelling about ten times heavier and more intense. . . .

One more note, a short one, written next morning:

. . . the BBC bulletins yesterday a bit disquieting — Arras, Cambrai and Amiens in enemy hands. . . . I wonder if there's a good hatch of mayfly on the Mole.

After that, silence.

The River Mole is a tributary of the Thames. Alfred's home was near Stoke d'Abernon in Surrey, a charming old farmhouse called Sheepbell. Like all the Savills, Alfred was a keen and skilful fisherman, and he was fortunate to have a trout stream within minutes of his door. The land falls away east of Sheepbell and the Mole meanders lazily down the valley through Leatherhead, Fetcham, past the ancient manor house at Slyfield, and on to Cobham. Early in 1940, while on leave, he had invited an old friend, an inept angler, to fish his water during the coming season when he got the chance.

It was at the beginning of June in the same year. The weather was perfect, the level of the water just right and, as it happened, there was an exceptionally large hatch of mayfly. But everything was spoiled, for it was the second week of the retreat to Dunkirk. People were going about their business tense, tight-lipped, ominously quiet; apart from that one dreadful subject there was really nothing to talk about. From the peaceful Surrey country-side those terrible happenings seemed infinitely remote except when there came, borne over the still air, the distant thunder of guns.

The time passed slowly. The gunfire ceased and we were told on the wireless that most of our troops were back. They were granted leave and made their way to their homes, alone or in twos and threes – but not Alfred. They had said there were yet a few to come. Was there still hope?

Such were the thoughts of the inept angler on the river bank. It was a warm, sunny afternoon and a cloudless sky was mirrored in the water save when a breeze ruffled the surface. Incautious mayfly voyaged downstream like tiny ships under sail. A trout, rising greedily in the pool above the alders, attracted the angler's attention – but he was not in the mood.

Half-heartedly he made a cast. It was a bad one, neither long enough nor straight. He cast again and it was worse. A third attempt, almost angrily, was disastrous. Inept angler indeed! A voice from behind him:

'Don't be such a bloody fool. Wade out into the stream and have a go from there; you'll never reach him from where you are. . . .'

Yes, it was Alfred, his wife beside him – Alfred looking very tired, in a creased and muddy uniform. On getting home he had hurried to the river. *Was the mayfly still up?* The three dined that evening at a kindly old inn in Cobham. It was wartime, but they dined well.

The rest of the story can be told quite shortly. During the retreat he had commanded his battery with great gallantry, for which he was awarded the DSO. He was promoted Lieutenant-Colonel in July of the same year and given command of the 53rd Anti-Tank Regiment. But he never returned to France. He was posted to various parts of the country and declined to spare himself. In January 1941 he had his first spell in hospital, and a few weeks later a second; gradually his health deteriorated. Major-General Otto Lund said of him: 'It was in my opinion the untiring efforts of Lieutenant-Colonel Savill, despite frequent illness, that put his regiment among the most efficient in the Artillery . . . he had at times more or less to be ordered to report sick.' The authorities conceded that if his illness was not solely attributable to military service, it had been aggravated and hastened by all he had been through during two world wars. He died on 17 September 1943 in his 46th year.

HENRY NORMAN SAVILL
1874–1945

EDWIN LYDALL SAVILL

1894–1940

LIEUT.-COL. ALFRED CECIL SAVILL DSO MC
1897–1943

SIR ERIC HUMPHREY SAVILL, KCVO CBE MC
born 1895
in the Savill Garden, Windsor Great Park
By courtesy of the Harry Smith Horticultural Photographic Collection

IO

Postwar chronicle

*Norman Savill's death (1945) – and Edwin's (1947) –
a personal note – John Loscombe Lydall Savill (Gen. X,
b. 1917) – first postwar Labour government – Agriculture
Act 1947 – Town and Country Planning Act 1947 –
coming of the New Towns – John Watson (b. 1903) –
Lands Tribunal – 'Battle of Crichel Down'*

Germany surrendered unconditionally to the Allies on 8 May
1945, and Japan on 14 August. But in the offices of Alfred Savill
and Sons any celebration of the return of peace was dimmed by
the death of Norman Savill on 15 September. His elder brother
Edwin, in retirement, was to die on 11 September two years later.
They were the third and fifth sons of Alfred Savill of Chigwell
Hall. The death of the fourth son, Robert Cecil, in 1952, marked
the passing of the eighth generation of Savills beginning with
Henry Savill who married Elizabeth Swallow at Great Dunmow
in 1652. It may be of interest to consider briefly, and to an extent
contrast, the qualities of the two brothers who were partners
for so many years.

Edwin and Norman were alike in some ways, but unlike in
others. Both were forthright and assertive of opinions they did
not always share. Both had charm and a spontaneous gaiety that
could be captivating. Both were receptive, witty and likable.
Both were kind. Both enjoyed the company of young people.

Edwin's marriage failed, as did Norman's first marriage.
Edwin, however, had three sons and brought them all into the
family business. Norman had two daughters, but until later in
life no son. He dwelt on that misfortune, and one discerns beneath
the gaiety a craving for affection and a loneliness which marred

his middle years. But it was in their approach to the business that they differed most. Edwin's work was a vocation; he found it absorbing, at times exciting, and all his boundless energy was applied to it. Norman by contrast was an intellectual; but for an insistent father he would probably have followed some other profession. A little group of surveyors, all of whom had been Norman Savill's pupils, were discussing their former master. One said: 'I was devoted to him.' The others nodded assent.

Norman Savill's death, so soon after the deaths of his nephews, resulted in the firm of Alfred Savill and Sons having no Savill in the office for the first time. Henry (Gen. IX), Norman's son by his second marriage, was only 16 and still at Harrow.

Happily the situation was soon remedied. John Loscombe Lydall Savill, Lydall Savill's son by his first marriage, was nearly 28 when the war ended. John, although of Generation X, is ten years older than his cousin Henry of Generation IX. John had been educated at Radley and had taken a degree at Jesus College, Cambridge. For two years in succession he had rowed for Cambridge in the University Boat Race.

When war broke out in September 1939, he joned the Navy and served as ordinary seaman until the end of the year. Then he was commissioned in the Irish Guards and saw active service in north-west Europe. He was wounded, and demobilized with the rank of major in March 1946. Like Peter Laycock, he was awarded Le Croix de Guerre avec Palme (Belgium); he is also Chevalier de l'Ordre de Leopold II avec Palme (Belgium).

On coming out of the Army John Savill found himself at a loose end. He had read anthropology and geography at Cambridge, but had made no decision about a peace-time career. His father and uncle were dead, and Sir Edwin, his grandfather, was by now in his late seventies and in failing health. On 12 April 1946 he called on Conky Turner, then senior partner in Alfred Savill and Sons, at 51a Lincoln's Inn Fields.

There followed a talk with Turner and Jim Eve, and the upshot was an invitation to enter the office a few weeks later. To the joy of his grandfather, John accepted the invitation. He had passed the examinations of the Royal Institution of Chartered Surveyors by 1949 and in 1952 they took him into partnership. He interested himself in the rural side of the practice and retired in 1977. John Savill married, in 1953, Betty Constance, the only daughter of Samuel Mence of Middleton-on-Sea in Sussex. By her he has one son and two daughters; at the time of writing his son, Jolyon Robert Lydall Savill (Gen. XI, born 1958), has just left Pangbourne College.

Peter Laycock was demobilized in the autumn of 1945, and one by one the other members of the staff who had served in the armed forces came back. So did Douglas White from the National Fire Service; he had spent the war fighting fires in and around London and had mercifully survived the holocaust at Elephant and Castle.

Events since the end of the Second World War are too recent to be dignified by the description 'history'. But the older generation will remember, and the younger may have been told, that in July 1945 there was a general election. The Conservatives under Winston Churchill were defeated, and Labour under Clement Attlee was returned to power. In early August the atomic bomb was used against Japan, and Hiroshima and Nagasaki were laid waste with appalling casualties, and we have seen that on 14 August Japan surrendered unconditionally to the Allies. On 20 November the trial of war criminals opened in Nuremberg, although it was not until 16 October of the following year that the capital sentences on the convicted Nazis were carried out. The major criminals succeeded in escaping the gallows. Mussolini and his mistress had been shot by Italian partisans on 28 April 1945. Hitler killed himself and his mistress two days later; he was followed by Goebbels who destroyed his family and then himself. Goering stood his trial at Nuremberg and was convicted, and after being sentenced to be hanged took poison.

At home, in the meantime, the first Labour government for fourteen years were getting into their stride. They were beset with problems. Some people appeared to think that once an armistice had been signed, the evacuees had returned, the lights had been turned up, the bombs had stopped falling and the sirens wailing, things would quickly be back to normal. They were gravely mistaken. We were short of food for many months, consumer goods of all kinds unobtainable in wartime were slow to reappear in the shops, petrol continued to be rationed, and the rationing of clothing lasted until 1949. In the initial period no builder's work was permitted except for the urgent repair of war damage; there followed a period when all building was subject to licence and there were severe penalties for exceeding the authorized expenditure. Few new houses were built, and those built were mainly for agricultural workers.

To maintain the prosperity of the agricultural industry was a major concern of this first postwar government. How could it have been otherwise? Basically, there was no party-political issue. Because of a worldwide shortage of food, home production was still a vital consideration. No government, of whatever political complexion, would have risked a recurrence of the disaster which followed the First World War. A meeting, convened by the Royal Agricultural Society of England, was attended by nearly every agricultural organization in the country and presided over by a Conservative Member of Parliament. It resolved unanimously:

In return for a guaranteed price level, all owners and occupiers of rural land must accept an obligation to maintain a reasonable standard of good husbandry and good estate management, and submit to the necessary measure of direction and guidance, subject to provisions for appeal to an impartial tribunal.

That, in short, is what the Labour government's Agriculture Act of 1947 accomplished. Much of what it provided was a continuance of the wartime system. Farmers continued to be guaranteed minimum prices for all their main products. The county war agricultural executive committees were replaced by peace-time committees with similar powers. The government undertook to see that all agricultural land was adequately equipped and properly farmed. Farming landowners who farmed badly could be bought out, and inefficient tenants deprived of their tenancies; appeals lay to 'agricultural land tribunals'. All land acquired on behalf of the State, which was not needed for the time being for any other purpose, was to be farmed by a new offshoot of the Ministry of Agriculture, called the Agricultural Land Commission, staffed by experts.

But a spearhead of socialist policies is nationalization. The Labour Party, no longer inhibited by the political give-and-take inevitable in a coalition government, were eager to get on with it. The coal-mining industry was nationalized on 1 January 1947, and the railways precisely a year later. They also had their eye on the commercial development of land.

We have seen that for years a major tenet of the Liberals – witness the writings of John Stuart Mill and Henry George – had been that any capital profit made by developing land ought to be shared by the developer and the community; that the developer should receive payment for his expertise and a fair return on his capital; that the balance, which may be the lion's share, should accrue to the community. Lloyd George had gone some way towards establishing that principle in the 1909–10 Finance Act, but in the outcome had failed. In the meantime the principle had become embodied in socialist philosophy, and it is scarcely surprising that Attlee's government made a further attempt.

The Town and Country Planning Act 1932 had not accomplished all its sponsors hoped for. It is a fair criticism of interwar planning legislation that it dealt independently and piecemeal with a variety of related problems. For the purposes of postwar reconstruction there was need for a national and comprehensive, rather than a local, approach.

Three reports, all made in wartime at the instance of the coalition government, were the Barlow Report 1938 (Royal Commission on the Location of Industry), the Scott Report 1941–2 (Committee on the Utilization of Land in Rural Areas), and the Uthwatt Report 1941 (Expert Committee on Compensation and Betterment). Each in its way exercised a marked influence on the provisions of the Town and Country Planning Act of 1947. In spite of its imperfections, that Act was undoubtedly one of the most important measures concerning the land in the history of this country. Provisions since carried into effect included a new system of planning control through the medium of local authority development plans, subject to frequent reviews; the prohibition of any development (i.e. building on the land or changing its use) without planning permission; extended powers to local authorities to develop land and acquire it compulsorily for that purpose. Parts of the Act, which in the event never became fully operative, provided for expropriation by the State of the development rights in all land subject to compensation, and the subsequent levying of a 'development charge' (with exceptions) by the Central Land Board in respect of any form of development – and, as a corollary, the assessment of compensation for the compulsory acquisition of land and buildings at existing-use value.

Neither Barlow, Scott nor Uthwatt had recommended the nationalization of land – if only because it was outside their terms of reference. Nor did the Attlee government propose its nationalization. Part VI of the Act provided merely for the nationalization of development rights in land. It meant, however, once the Act was in force, that an owner would no longer have the right to develop his own land or change its use. He would only be permitted to continue using it for its existing purpose. The total development value of land in England and Wales had been estimated (no one except the experts knows how) at £300 millions on a global basis.* For the loss of their development rights owners were to be compensated in proportion to the value of their holdings up to that total.

Suppose, later, an owner who had been compensated for the loss of his development rights wanted to develop the land in question. After getting planning permission, he

---

*'Global value' may be explained in this way. A town is likely to expand but no one knows in which direction. Every landowner hopes the expansion will be in his direction, and all the land around the town acquires a 'hope value' in anticipation. The total global value is the total market value less an estimate of that part of the hope value that will not in the event be realized.

would have to buy or lease back his development rights at 100 per cent of their current value. The following is a simple illustration.

Mr Black owned a house and grounds with a road frontage ripe for development. At the appointed day their total value, with a right by the purchaser to build on the frontage, was £15,000; without that right, £12,000. The difference of £3,000 was the 'development value' and he would have a claim against the £300 million fund for the loss of it. At a later date he decided to develop the frontage himself or sell it for that purpose. The value of building land had risen in the meantime – but not because of anything done by Mr Black. The total value was now £17,000 of which £5,000 related to the road frontage. The 100 per cent development charge was accordingly £5,000. The 'unearned increment' of £2,000 went to the State and not to Mr Black.

These proposals met with approval far outside the Labour Party. They were at least logical and had the virtue of being simple. Development value that had accrued to a landowner before the appointed day belonged to him and was to be purchased from him; development value accruing thereafter was to belong to the community.

Before passing to other matters, reference must be made to another item of importance in the Attlee government's crowded legislative programme. The New Towns Act of 1946 was based on the recommendations of the New Towns (Reith) Committee that had been appointed the previous year.

A policy of planned decentralization from congested urban areas by the building of New Towns (known in early days as 'satellite towns' and 'garden cities') was not new. The pioneer was Sir Ebenezer Howard (1850–1928), author of *Garden Cities of Tomorrow* which was first published with the title *Tomorrow* in 1898. The first practical experiments were made by private enterprise, both in Hertfordshire. Letchworth Garden City was established in 1903 and Welwyn Garden City in 1921. Much was learned from these experiments. It was left to a Labour government, as part of their scheme for economic and social reconstruction after the Second World War, to develop Howard's conception on a national scale.

The first report of the Reith Committee had been mainly about 'agency' – that is to say, the nature of the body to be charged with responsibility for building a New Town and its subsequent management. There were several possibilities, but the committee favoured a government-sponsored corporation financed by the Exchequer. In two further reports the committee dealt with such matters as types of New Town (entirely new or an existing town enlarged), selection of site, size, social structure, public services, the process and order of residential and industrial development, the need for a variety of employment, health, facilities for education, social life and recreation.

The first New Towns Act was passed in the autumn of 1946 and the first of the New Towns, an extension of the existing town of Stevenage in Hertfordshire, was established in the same year. The New Towns policy has since been pursued by successive governments. Inevitably there have been unforeseen difficulties and consequent changes of plan and amendments of the 1946 Act. Credit must be given, however, to the first postwar Labour government for their imagination and foresight – even more, perhaps, for the speed with which they got down to the job. At December 1975 there were twenty-nine New Towns being developed under the New Towns Act in England and Wales and in Scotland, and four in Northern Ireland. In the twenty-nine, at that date, there were 325,958 new dwellings, 4,290 new shops, 3,129 new factories and 640 new schools; the total population was 929,179.

In 1946 the singular John Watson whom we mentioned earlier became a partner.* We recorded his association with Alfred Savill and Sons during the interwar period as a rating surveyor. In the meantime he had become interested in housing and housing management, and since 1940 had held a personal appointment

*See page 120.

as agent for the Marquess of Northampton's estates in North London. John Watson had also served on several governmental committees, including the Central Housing Advisory Committee (1936–47) and the New Towns (Reith) Committee (1945–6). During the war he had been chairman of the Conservative Party's Subcommittee on Housing, and was shortly to become a member of the Development Corporation of the New Town of Stevenage. He had also written books – and was destined to write more; their titles, *per curiam*, have strayed on to the flyleaf of this one.

As a partner in Alfred Savill and Sons, he was mainly concerned with rating. With the help of A. J. C. (Bertie) Dowden, later a partner, he founded what the firm had never had before – a rating surveyors' department. It found plenty to do; so much, in fact, that Watson was constrained to enlist the co-operation of J. H. Emlyn Jones, an experienced rating surveyor and a partner in Rees-Reynolds and Hunt, another firm of surveyors who practised in Lincoln's Inn Fields.

One of the earliest jobs undertaken was, and still is, the rating of the fuel stations and installations of Shell Mex BP* throughout England and Wales. That led to the rating of the Petrofina fuel stations and of the refineries belonging to Conoco and Lindsey Oils (Total/Fina) in Lincolnshire. Other industrial and commercial rating clients include Heinz, Imperial Tobacco, Beecham Foods, Babcock and Wilcox, Granada TV Rental, Horne Brothers, Mothercare and Harrods. And as rating surveyors to Trust House Forte, they are concerned with the assessments of restaurants, snack bars and service areas on half the motorways in the country.

In 1949 John Watson followed in the footsteps of Sir Edwin Savill by becoming President (session 1949–50) of the Royal Institution of Chartered Surveyors. In his Opening Address, 'The Spirit of a Profession', he discussed a matter we touched on in connection with the attitude adopted by its council towards

*Now Shell UK Oil, BP Oil and National Benzol.

Lloyd George's People's Budget - the importance of a professional society keeping aloof from party politics:

A chartered surveyor, like any other subject, is fully entitled to his own opinions of what is right and wrong. . . . On political issues, as on individual, he is entitled to express them with that freedom which Milton ranked 'above all liberties'. That he may do from the platform of the Fabian Society or of the Primrose League - both honourable bodies - according to his way of thinking. But he must not expect his professional society, comprising, as it does some 16000 members of all shades of political opinion, to take sides. To do so would be to imperil that structure of public confidence in our profession which has been built up by our forbears over more than eighty years. No longer, if an acknowledged partisan, would the Institution command the respect and retain the ear of successive governments.

Towards the end of his Address he spoke to the younger members of his audience on the subject of service:

Ich dien! The finest tradition of any calling is a readiness to serve. The spirit of a great profession is the spirit of service. It is a spirit that must govern our approach to every question, for it is active in all sections of our membership, in all branches, and at all ages. . . . It is a spirit which derives, I suggest, from an interest not in things but in people - which alone begets understanding. And the gift of understanding, you will recall, was the first among all gifts which that great architect, King Solomon, prayed for. I say to you most earnestly - the younger members of the profession - maintain that tradition.

John Watson was never more than an associate partner in Alfred Savill and Sons. He had too many irons in the fire and has described himself as an 'incompleat surveyor'. At the age of 32 he became a magistrate and at 33 a chairman of the Inner London (formerly Metropolitan) juvenile courts. He was a member of the Royal Commission on Justices of the Peace (1946-8) and thereafter went to Germany to advise the Control Commission on problems arising from juvenile delinquency in the British Zone and in Berlin. Obviously he was unable to devote as much time to his professional practice as a full-time partnership would have demanded.

An important measure, passed in his year of office as President of the Royal Institution of Chartered Surveyors, was the Lands Tribunal Act of 1949. The newly formed tribunal took over the work of the official arbitrators, who had sat mainly to determine disputes about the amount of compensation payable for compulsory acquisitions. The Lands Tribunal, however, has a wider jurisdiction and heavier responsibilities. It consists of as many members as the Lord Chancellor sees fit to appoint. The president of the tribunal must be a barrister who has held a judicial office or is at least of seven years' standing. The other members are barristers or solicitors, and persons experienced in the valuation of land and buildings; they are commonly referred to as the 'lawyer' members and 'valuer' members respectively. Membership is a whole-time job and the member generally sits alone; the tribunal is part of the judiciary. At the time of writing there are two lawyer members and six valuer members.

Under the 1949 Act the Lord Chancellor, before appointing a valuer member, is required to consult the president for the time being of the Royal Institution of Chartered Surveyors. It fell to John Watson to make the first batch of recommendations. In 1956 he himself was made a member of the Lands Tribunal; and so ended a partnership in Alfred Savill and Sons that had lasted nine happy years.

Some three years before his retirement the firm was involved in a fracas down in Dorset. Local to begin with, concerning a few hundred acres, it was adjudged before it ended a national scandal. In retrospect, some might describe it as a regrettable controversy; others as a splendid row which did a power of good. It all depends on the point of view.

The average Englishman is too complacent. Should he suffer injustice, he complains and protests. But if the channelling of his protests into positive action threatens to involve him in time, expense, obloquy and possibly hatred, he is prone to submit. Happily there are exceptions. John Hampden was one. In a

more democratic society, Lieutenant-Commander George Marten
RN of Crichel in the County of Dorset, a client of Jim Eve, was
another.

The full story of Crichel Down, the arbitrary methods of
certain officials, a public inquiry, a scathing report and finally
the resignation of the responsible Minister, are outside the ambit
of this book. The following is a bare statement of the facts.

Crichel Down extends to 725 acres; before the war it was
partly arable but mostly sheep grazing. 328 acres had belonged to
Lord Alington who, when he died in 1940, left his estate in trust
for his daughter who later married Lieutenant-Commander
Marten. But not those 328 acres. In 1937 they had been acquired
compulsorily by the Air Ministry, together with the rest of the
Down, for the purpose of a bombing range. In 1949, because they
no longer wanted it, the Air Ministry transferred the land to the
Ministry of Agriculture. The Minister entrusted its management
to the Agricultural Land Commission which we have mentioned;
the commission delegated that duty to the Land Service, another
recent offshoot of the Ministry; and the Land Service relied on the
Dorset Agricultural Executive Committee. It fell to these bodies,
which were staffed by civil servants, to advise the Minister what
should be done with the land in question.

Various suggestions were made and debated, but only two
courses were considered to be practicable. One was to let Crichel
Down in blocks to neighbouring farmers; the other, to equip
it for farming as a single unit (at a cost variously estimated at
between £18,500 and £40,000) and find a suitable tenant.

In law, there was a third course which these gentlemen ignored,
if at that time they were aware of it: to advise the Minister to sell
the land for farming under powers conferred on him by Section
90 of the Agriculture Act 1947. Their disregard of this third course
was never explained satisfactorily. In the event, they decided in
favour of the second – to equip the land and let it as a whole.
They contended that to do so would be in the best interests of
food production; it would be a model farm and, as was said later,
farming it would be 'a very interesting experience'. One civil

servant, highly placed, was asked in cross-examination at the public inquiry: 'Would it be fair to say that you thought it would be rather fun?' He replied: 'No, I do not think it would be fair to say that. ...'

The Minister of Agriculture was advised accordingly. It was surprising advice in the light of applications that had been made to rent the land in its existing condition, which on the face of them seemed a better financial proposition. One of the earliest and most persistent applicants had been Lieutenant-Commander Marten, who wanted to buy the land as it was and so regain possession of what had once been part of his wife's family estate. The 'Battle of Crichel Down', as it came to be called, was the outcome of the combined efforts of the civil servants to prevent his doing so.

It ended, as we have said, in a public inquiry. No suggestion was made of any sort of corruption. There was, however, overwhelming evidence of incompetence, obstinacy and smugness. Basic facts had not been apprehended; estimates had been conflicting; secrecy had been enjoined unnecessarily; a report to a Minister was 'riddled with inaccuracies'; applications had been staved off without being given proper consideration. Commander Marten had been deemed a nuisance.

'A nuisance' – and why not? Commander Marten was not the sort of man to take this lying down. He wrote letters to officials and attended conferences. All his letters were not answered and the conferences proved abortive. He invaded the Ministry and complained personally to Mr Nugent, the Parliamentary Secretary who had been handling the matter. He enlisted the support of his Member of Parliament, Mr Crouch. He convened meetings and wrote letters to the press – all to no avail. The final straw was when the Minister agreed to sell Crichel Down to the Commissioners of Crown Lands subject to a tenancy that had been negotiated privately; no one else had had a chance to compete.

At the last moment Commander Marten secured an interview with the Minister himself, Sir Thomas Dugdale. But Sir Thomas was unresponsive, and anyhow it was too late. The owners of no less than 167,000 acres then petitioned for an inquiry and the national newspapers became full of it. The Minister was left with no alternative, and a public inquiry was ordered.

The inquirer was Sir Andrew Clark QC, and Jim Eve gave evidence for Lieutenant-Commander Marten. Sir Andrew, in his report dated June 1954, spared no one and some of his criticisms of officialdom were devastating. It may be thought, however, that this moderate passaged summed it up:

The Land Commission was a comparatively new body, very anxious to gain experience by trying their hand at a new and interesting venture . . . and, in their eagerness to ensure that they were not deprived of the opportunity, they adopted an irresponsible attitude to the expenditure of public money, and they were not always as frank with the Minister as they might have been,

In Parliament, the Minister very properly accepted responsibility for the errors of his advisers, and after expressing regret resigned his office. Thereafter the government gave an undertaking which has ever since been honoured: agricultural land that has been acquired compulsorily by a government department which the State wants to dispose of, must be offered first to the original owner; should he not buy it, it must be offered at auction. In the Civil Service, at the expense of well-intentioned gentlemen who must have regretted their indiscretions, a lesson had been learned. In Dorset, Crichel Down was sold to the Martens and is again an integral part of their estate.

I I

This modern age

Background of events – town planning again, mend and make do – changes in the firm – Henry Edward Savill (Gen. IX, b. 1929) – 'Savills' – a visit to head office – Land Commission 1967 – Community Land Act 1975 – Development Land Tax Act 1976 – property investment today – institutions as investors – farming partnerships – the indestructible asset

While this was going on down in Dorset, important things had been happening elsewhere. A Conservative government under Winston Churchill had been in office since 1951. King George VI had died (February 1952) and been succeeded by his elder daughter Queen Elizabeth II. The setting up of the European Defence Community had been approved by Parliament (August 1952). Tea had come off the ration (October 1952), sweets (February 1953), all remaining foodstuffs (July 1954). Queen Mary had died (March 1953). Hillary and Hunt had climbed Everest (May 1953). In the meantime experts had identified a fish caught off Madagascar as a species of the prehistoric coelacanth; even if the excitement at this discovery was dimmed on the discovery by other experts that the skull of the Piltdown Man, unearthed in Sussex in 1911 and acclaimed conclusive evidence of our descent from apes, was in fact a fraud.

More relevant to our theme had been the publication of a White Paper, in November 1952, entitled *Proposals for amending the Financial Provisions of the Town and Country Planning Act 1947.** The Conservatives had always disliked those provisions.

*Part VI.

Their proposals, among others, were to abolish development charges and to suspend the distribution of the £300 millions to successful claimants for the acquisition of their development rights, which were due to be made in two years' time. These repeals were effected by the Town and Country Planning Act of 1953, which came on the heels of the White Paper.

A major objection by the Conservative Party to the financial provisions of the 1947 Act had been on the ground that the £300 million fund was inadequate. Another objection, which in the event proved justified, was to a development charge of 100 per cent of the development value. The State had been too greedy. How much more sensible, said the critics of the Labour government, if the percentage had been made variable from place to place and from time to time – low in one area where there was need to encourage development, high in another where it had been overdone. The 100 per cent charge gave no incentive to the landowner to provide the developer's raw material, and it was scarcely surprising that many owners held on to their land rather than put it on the market.

There are those who believe that the repeal of these provisions of the Town and Country Planning Act 1947 was a grave mistake. The Act had been passed at the ideal time, when little building was in progress and the postwar planning situation was still flexible. They contend that by constructive amendment it could have been made to work, in which case many of our subsequent planning problems might not have arisen.

Be that as it may, the repeal of part of an Act inevitably leaves loose ends that have to be tied up. That happened here, and it may be thought it was not accomplished very effectively. There were many anomalies too complicated with which to burden the reader. The Town and Country Planning Acts of 1954, 1959, 1962 and 1963 were attempts to resolve them. It should be noted, however, that during the life of this government – or indeed of any later Conservative government – there was no attempt to re-enact the 1947 Act provisions for the compulsory acquisition of development rights even in modified form.

At a general election in October 1964 Labour came back under Harold Wilson. They had been biding their time, and the opportunity for a further effort towards a 'betterment levy' had arrived.

The Land Commission Act of 1967 received Royal Assent on 1 February 1967. It provided for a levy on development value, when realized as a result of any of the following 'chargeable acts or events':

Sale of land (vendor to pay levy);

Leasing of land (lessor to pay levy);

Development begun after 6 April 1967 (developer to pay levy;)

Receipt of compensation for refusal, modification or revocation of planning permission (recipient to pay levy);

Granting an easement or releasing a restrictive covenant (grantor to pay levy);

Certain minor happenings.

The Land Commission, having been notified, were to serve a 'notice of assessment'; the amount of the assessment to be agreed if possible between the person chargeable, or his professional advisers, and the Inland Revenue valuer. If that were not possible, an appeal lay to the Lands Tribunal. Once the assessment had been fixed, the levy began at 40 per cent of the 'net development value'; the government, however, had made it clear that this would shortly be raised to 45 per cent and eventually to 50 per cent.

Part II of the Act empowered the Land Commission to acquire, manage and dispose of land – the intention being that the commission itself should play an active part in bringing forward ripe land for development. Between 1967 and 1970 the commission bought and disposed of a few small areas, but its more ambitious plans did not materialize.

The Land Commission Act was repealed by the Conservative government under Edward Heath, which came into power in 1970. Apart from any political considerations, a valid reason for its repeal was that the high cost of assessing and collecting betterment had proved out of proportion to the comparatively small amount collected. And an absurdity had arisen from the interpretation of 'development', which included a preliminary operation as trifling as digging a trench. Prospective developers rushed to dig trenches before 6 April 1967 and thereby escape the levy. Little further development, which would attract the levy, was begun until long afterwards.

The amount of work that fell to professional valuers under these enactments was enormous, and most of it abortive. At about the time that the Town and Country Planning Act 1947 came into operation, Patrick Maslen joined Alfred Savill and Sons as an associate partner. He had been in the Valuation Office of the Inland Revenue all his life, and had lately retired from the important office of Superintending Valuer for the London Area. The firm's clients, concerned to obtain fair settlements of their various claims, were fortunate in having on their side a valuer with such long experience in arguing from the opposite side of the fence.

As a result of John Watson's resignation in 1956 on appointment to the Lands Tribunal, someone had to be found to take charge of the rating department. The obvious choice was J. H. Emlyn Jones, a partner in Rees-Reynolds and Hunt, the very experienced rating surveyor with whom, as we mentioned earlier, the firm had already formed an asssociation. The senior partner in Rees-Reynolds and Hunt was H. R. J. (Richard) Webster, son of the late Sir Hugh Webster, the official arbitrator. Richard was a contemporary of Peter Laycock and had been articled to Sir Edwin Savill. One of his most interesting appointments was, and still is, the surveyorship to Chelsea Royal Hospital. That famous institution, home of ageing and disabled soldiers known affectionately as 'Chelsea pensioners', was founded by Charles II in 1682; its architect and first surveyor was Sir Christopher Wren.

The reader will have noted, as the years went by, how the business founded by Jonathan Savill in the early nineteenth century had widened its scope. His son, Alfred Savill, became agent for great estates and an acknowledged authority on manorial land tenure. Edwin Savill broke new ground by developing the urban side of the practice. An amalgamation with Rees-Reynold and Hunt, with effect from January 1957, marked a further stage in the widening process. That firm's office was at 63 Lincoln's Inn Fields. They were not only rating surveyors, but specialist advisers on commercial property investment, and that was a direction in which Alfred Savill and Sons were minded to expand. Initially the combined firm worked from the two offices, but when the whole of no. 63 became available in 1965 they moved their headquarters there.

During the next ten years there were several changes in the partnership, besides minor amalgamations of which two were in East Anglia. In 1968 the Lord Chancellor appointed Emlyn Jones to the Lands Tribunal, and like John Watson he had to resign. Happily it was not before Bertie Dowden had become qualified to take over the rating. George Eve, still active as a consultant to the firm, died in 1959 in his 80th year. Fred Ragg, who had succeeded the third Alfred Savill as surveyor to the Leathersellers' Company, died in 1964; Patrick Maslen had died a few years earlier. A further loss was by the sudden death in 1957 of Ritchie Phillips, senior valuer, who had been Sir Edwin Savill's principal assistant. In the meantime, however, new young partners were admitted and the names of others, formerly members of the associated firms, appeared for the first time on the notepaper.

Henry Edward Savill (Gen. IX, *b.* 13 March 1929) joined the firm in 1953 and was taken into partnership in 1963. Henry, as we have recorded, is the only son of Norman Savill (Gen. VIII, 1874–1945) by his second wife, Jean Gill, whom he married in 1928. Henry had been educated at Harrow and Trinity College, Cambridge. He married in 1955 Gillian, only daughter of Roger Kemsley of Theydon Bois in Essex, by whom he has three sons (Generation X): Norman Hugh (*b.* 30 July 1957), Cecil Henry (*b.* 2 March 1965) and Benjamin Edward (*b.* 1 August 1968).

In 1967 Alfred Savill and Sons amalgamated with Curtis and Henson, an old-established firm of surveyors, land and estate agents, who had their head office in the West End of London and a country office at Banbury. Curtis and Henson had long experience in the sale and purchase of residential property. They had in addition a practice in agricultural estate management, comparable to that of Alfred Savill and Sons, and had strong connections with 'institutional' clients; they shared the interest shown by those clients in agricultural land as an investment – a comparatively new departure to which we shall return presently. There were at that time six partners in Curtis and Henson, of whom two – Cecil Feilden and Arthur Salter – have since retired. The other four – Jeremy Wilson, Henry Douglas-Pennant, Tony Harris and Michael Stourton – are partners in the composite firm which in 1972 took the name 'Savills'.

In 1972 the firm established its present head office at 20 Grosvenor Hill in the City of Westminster. When they moved Jim Eve, who had succeeded Conky Turner, was head of it. Jim retired in 1974 to become a consultant and was succeeded by Richard Webster as senior partner.

Not long since, one of our more inquisitive readers secured an invitation to Savill's head office on Grosvenor Hill. They received him cordially. He admired in turn the simple façade of the modern functional building, the murals in the entrance hall, the pretty girl at the reception desk and the semi-tropical arboretum alongside her. He was introduced to several partners and to Charles Port, that venerable head of the general office, whose duty it is to keep the staff as well as the partners in order. The virtues of an 'open-plan' office layout were explained to him. Thereafter he inspected many and allegedly different departments, no one of which – even where it begins or ends – can be distinguished from any other. Eventually they escorted him back to the entrance hall, whence, after a hopeful smile towards the arboretum, he made his way out.

But a visit to Savills was not enough. It was still only five o'clock and further entertainment was called for. He pondered for a few minutes. Then he walked the length of Berkeley Street, through the Royal Parks, skirted Parliament Square and arrived unexpectedly in the House of Commons.

That second visit was a flop. No impassioned rhetoric, no scintillating wit, no penetrating thrusts, no reprimands by the Speaker, not a single Member suspended. The Chamber was only a quarter full and the Strangers' Gallery almost empty. The subject under discussion was the 'Land Bill' – and whether it was the Community Land Bill of 1975, or the Development Land Tax Bill of 1976, is of no consequence. A lot of what they said was inaudible; most of what was audible was unintelligible; and all that was intelligible was unutterably tedious. He was a witness, willy-nilly, of the Labour Party's most recent attempt to capture betterment.

This was the Labour government of Harold Wilson which had come into office in March 1974. A few months before that happened Edward Heath, Prime Minister in the preceding Conservative government, had reacted belatedly to a public outcry against the excessive profits being made by speculative property developers notwithstanding the incidence of capital gains tax. He had departed so far from traditional Tory principles as to promise some new form of development tax. Then came a general election, after which, ironically, it fell to Labour to introduce it.

The new government's proposals were contained in the Finance Act 1974. Until then, capital gains tax (at 30 per cent) had been payable on the development of land and buildings only when they came to be sold. In future, any increase in value due to development was to be split between 'development gain' and 'capital gain'. The first was to be treated as part of the developer's income and be subject to income tax under Schedule D; the second was to continue to attract capital gains tax.

Then had come two White Papers in which the government made known their further intentions. Local authorities were to be required to buy compulsorily all the land they considered ought to be developed during the ensuing ten years, and there was to be a new tax on profits from commercial development to be called 'development land tax'. These proposals had had a dual purpose. First, they would enable the community to plan the development of land according to its needs and priorities;

second, they would ensure that the bulk of any profit arising from development would accrue to the community and not to the developer.

The tedious debate, to which our reader was constrained to listen in Parliament, was the forerunner of the legislation to attain these objects. The Community Land Act received Royal Assent in November 1975, and its sister-measure, the Development Land Tax Act, in July 1976. Both are current at the time of writing.

The Community Land Act 1975 laid down a timetable. There are to be three periods, the initial period, a transitional period and the final period.

During the initial period local authorities are to be *empowered* to acquire land they consider will be needed for development. In the final period they will be *required* to do so. The transitional period may be as long as ten years or even longer; while it lasts, the complex provisions of the Act will gradually come into force and local authority purchases will be at market value less development land tax at varying rates. Only in the final period will the Act be fully operative; purchases will be at current-use value, and development land tax will then become obsolete.

The Development Land Tax Act is the second leg of this legislation. 'Development' means, in brief, any development of land and buildings which either comprises building on a vacant site, or enlarges the cubic content of existing buildings by more than 10 per cent (called the 'tolerance'), or substantially changes the use of land or buildings. Initially, the developer may have to pay in tax up to 80 per cent of his profit, and it has been forecast that the maximum will be increased by stages until it reaches 100 per cent. The nationalization of development values in land, subject to certain exemptions, will then be complete. Charities will be exempted, and the exemption from capital gains tax of one owner-occupied house per person will apply to development land tax. There will also be exemption from development land tax on a gain not exceeding £10,000 and a reduced rate of tax on the next £150,000.

We make no apologies for the shortness of this summary. For one thing, the provisions of these Acts are extremely complicated For another, the Conservative Opposition are pledged to repeal the Community Land Act (but not necessarily, in principle, the Development Land Tax Act) if and when they return to power.

Firms of surveyors and land agents have to consider what repercussions, if any, this legislation is likely to have on the property market. In this connection it is pertinent to recall what has been happening in that market since the end of the last war.

The factor which has dominated the scene resulted from the creation of the Welfare State. There has been a vast increase in the amount of money available for investment by pension funds and similar institutions, which today form an essential part of the salary structure, and in the case of the nationalized undertakings is virtually state-controlled. A substantial part of this money finds its way into the property market.

The legislation we have summarized, preceded by a series of measures which afforded greater security to tenants besides restricting rents, has affected the market in various ways. It has upset the process of free bargaining between landlord and tenant, and traditional methods of valuing are outdated. Statutory assumptions have to be made, at their best speculative and at their worst ridiculous. Fundamentally, however, the function of the professional valuer remains the same: from month to month, from week to week, sometimes from day to day, to interpret the vacillations of the market for the benefit of his client.

Today the range of investors in the property market is little different from that on the Stock Exchange. Institutional investors are no longer confined to traditional constituents of the Establishment such as the Crown, the Church, universities and charities; recent entrants may be described compendiously as 'the City' – life assurance offices, pension and superannuation funds, unit trusts and the like. All these are now in competition for sound commercial and/or agricultural investments as they become available. Special considerations apply to agricultural investments and we shall consider these presently.

An investor's object is to obtain the best possible combination of a secure covenant, a reasonable prospect of future increases in rent, and an adequate return on capital in the meantime. Extraneous circumstances can affect interest rates in the property market in the same way as in the stock market, and the property market is inured to booms and slumps. The obvious difference between the two classes of investment is that the property investor buys a visible asset, compared with a relatively small share in a corporate and invisible undertaking.

At one time property investments by institutions normally took the form of ground rents or mortgages. The next stage was when they began to favour 'created investments'; that is to say, freehold or leasehold properties already let, or which are about to be let and become income producing. Then, in the 1960s and 1970s, the institutions took to financing property companies. One method of doing that was to lend at a fixed rate of interest in return for an option on a specified number of ordinary shares at the price obtaining at the date of the loan – the institution thus acquiring a share in the equity. Another method, preferred by some developers, was to sell on what is known as the 'lease-back' basis. While the site was still being developed, the institution undertook to buy the completed building and thereafter lease it back to the developer at a head-rent equal to an agreed percentage of the purchase price. Should the developer, by his expertise, be able to negotiate subleases at rents which in total exceeded the head-rent, the 'top slice' of the leasehold interest belonged to him. Traders, too, took advantage of the lease-back arrangement; they were able to release their capital by selling their freehold, but remain in occupation as tenants of the purchasers.

The classes of property most popular with institutional investors are offices and shops in what the estate agents call 'prime' positions, and modern factories and warehouses. Residential properties, at the time of writing, are not in great demand. But the investor in commercial property does not always insist on the cream. In the inner suburbs of great cities and in the centres of smaller ones are offices and shops well let and well situated;

the security for rent is adequate and the yield on capital is higher.

We return to the question posed just now. What effect will current legislation have on the commercial property market? On the *bona fide* investor, it may be thought, very little. He is concerned with an existing building and its current use, and he buys the building at its current value. Provided any development he undertakes does not exceed the statutory 10 per cent of cubic content, or involve a substantial change in use, development land tax will not arise. The speculator, on the other hand, needs to be wary. We have in mind, for example, the dealer in land who gambles on a change of use to realize a big profit. We suggest his days are numbered, and no one is likely to grieve about that.

We turn now to investment in agricultural land. Like these other forms of property investment, it has suffered from the vagaries of legislation since the end of the Second World War. One government, intent on stimulating the agricultural industry, has made tax concessions to the landowner. The next government has modified them, replaced them by something different, or repealed them. One is inclined to wonder whether certain incidental consequences of some of the recent legislation concerning tax were foreseen.

Consider, for example, the incidence of current taxation in relation to the landowner who hopes to pass on his property to his heir, not only intact but under his heir's expert management. Gifts and bequests by husbands to wives and *vice versa* are free from tax. But when gifts are made to children they attract capital gains tax as well as capital transfer tax; should an owner give the estate to his heir, there is no escape from either. The latter's total liability to tax, arising from a gift compared with a bequest, is liable to vary between one estate and another. When the financial considerations favour a bequest, the owner will be tempted to hold on until he dies, which is unproductive of youthful enthusiasm. It should be noted, however, that gifts *inter vivos* not exceeding £100000 in value are chargeable to capital transfer tax at half the rate that would apply to assets passing on death, and that there are smaller concessions in respect of gifts between £100,000 and £300,000.

A repeal that adversely affected the landowner was effected in part by the Finance Act of 1962 and finally by that of 1964. Formerly, if he farmed the land himself and did so at a loss, he had been permitted to set that loss against income from other sources in calculating his taxable income. Take, for example, the home farm. At one time it was often farmed by the owner personally as a hobby. Some owners pursued a selective breeding policy and bred fine strains of horses, ponies, cattle or sheep. The owner was proud of his home farm and, thanks to this concession, indifferent to whether it made a profit or a loss. The concession was rescinded. Yet to let the home farm, which is an amenity to the residence if kept in hand, is nearly always a mistake. Should the estate be sold, the price it makes may be substantially reduced as a result of having done so.

The same applies today to the estate generally. The market value of agricultural land with the benefit of vacant possession has always been higher than if let and sold as an investment. The gap between the values has widened over the years, owing to an ever-increasing security of tenure afforded by the legislature to sitting tenants. Landowners, if they want to maintain the value of their properties, have come to recognize the importance of taking and keeping in hand as much land as they can.

There are still, however, unique advantages to be had from the ownership of agricultural land, *provided* the owner farms it himself, or has it farmed for him, or farms it in partnership. It is vital that in the eyes of the law he ranks as a *bona fide* farmer; whatever arrangements he may make, it is the responsibility of his professional advisers to make sure he has that status. Under the Finance Act 1975, as amended, the executors of a *bona fide* farmer, in respect of land not exceeding a thousand acres or worth more than a quarter of a million pounds (whichever limit is more favourable to the estate), may claim half of its agricultural value for the purpose of capital transfer tax; they may also claim relief of 30 per cent of the value of land over those limits, and of the value of live and dead stock if they are occupied or used in connection with the business.

The tax benefits that derive from farming land, as opposed to letting it, are not confined to capital taxes. A farmer is not liable for the 15 per cent 'investment' surcharge which is levied on the non-farming landowner. Thus by farming his own land an owner, who would otherwise pay away in tax 98 per cent of his income, can reduce the proportion paid away to 83 per cent.

To a landowner, not a professional farmer, who wishes to take advantage of these concessions, three courses are open. The first is to employ a firm of land agents to farm the land on his behalf, the second is to farm it in partnership with a professional farming company. The third is to farm it in partnership with an individual farmer or farmers.

In Chapter 2 we described a comparatively recent development of the traditional business of estate management known as 'farm management'. We pointed out that the landowner, relieved of trouble and anxiety, is still legally a farmer in occupation. A partnership, between the owner and a professional farming company or an individual farmer, must permit the owner to dissolve at such reasonably short notice as may be agreed. Although there is no generally accepted formula for the agreement, all such partnerships must be subject to four basic conditions: first, that the landowner shall receive an annual payment equivalent to rent; second, that the working partners shall receive payment for their effort and expertise equivalent to salary; third, that each partner shall receive interest on his capital, be it equity or loan capital; fourth, that any 'super-profit' shall be shared by the partners in proportion to the equity capital each has invested.

So much for the private investor in agricultural land. We have noted a shift in recent years to the institutional investor, and there is much to be said for this development in the interests of the rural community. Ample capital is available for improvements, and investment managers are fully conscious of their responsibilities. They rely on their valuer/land agent to find a suitable investment in the first place, negotiate its purchase, and handle any subsequent operations.

The primary purpose is to create a hedge against inflation. If the institution has confidence in the vendor, the purchase is sometimes effected on the lease-back basis that we have described. The arrangements can benefit both parties. The new owner can count on getting his rent from an experienced farmer, who knows all there is to know about the land in question, and is saved the trouble of having to find a new tenant; and continuity, an important factor in husbandry, is assured. The former owner has his capital released and continues farming the land, possibly as joint tenant with one or more of his sons who hope to succeed him.

It is true that the rapid growth which the institutions hoped for, when they bought agricultural land in the early 1970s, proved illusory. Values rose for a time – then fell. At the time of writing they are rising again; the value of agricultural land is inherently volatile. Capital growth is still an attraction for the City, but in the meantime, because of the continuing decline in the value of money, yields are also important. Lately the institutions have addressed their minds to finding some way by which the income from agricultural land can be increased. They are alive to the widening gap between vacant-possession value and investment value which we mentioned earlier. As in the case of the private landowner, there is everything to be said for having as much land in hand as possible, and one way of achieving it is to buy land affording vacant possession whenever an opportunity arises. But land in hand has to be farmed, and what does the City know about that?

We end our story with this final reference to the soil. It is as it should be; we declared at the outset that that was the background against which we should tell it. The Savills are an old English family, husbandry is our most ancient industry, the soil is our one indestructible asset. We have traced the descendants of Henry and Elizabeth of Little Easton over three centuries and through their ten generations. The limb of the family that concerns us has meantime thriven, burgeoned and put forth many branches; in the words of Ecclesiastes – 'One generation passeth away and another generation cometh.'

The firm called Savills is comparatively young, but it too has thriven. Today fifty-eight partners operate its head office and fifteen country offices in England and Wales. The offices are in five groups, each administered from a group office: London from head office; West Country from Wimborne; Midlands from Banbury; Norfolk from Norwich; Essex from Chelmsford. There is an asscoation with firms covering Scotland, and there are related Savill offices in Amsterdam and Paris. . . . A long haul, it may be thought, from the one-man business of Jonathan Savill, 'architect, builder, land agent and surveyor', who in 1836 valued one rood, thirty-six poles in the parish of Chigwell for the Right Reverend Father in God, Charles James, Lord Bishop of London.

THE SAVILLS

A Skeleton Pedigree
showing male descendants of
HENRY AND ELIZABETH SAVILL
m. at Great Dunmow
March 1652
(*Name in capitals denotes a principal in the firm*)

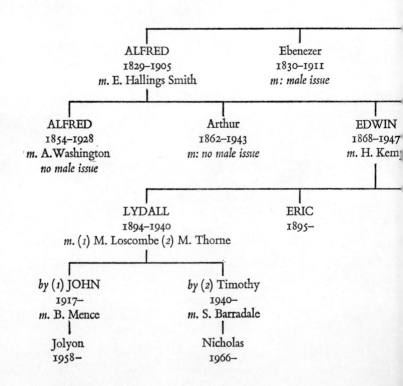

ALFRED
1829–1905
m. E. Hallings Smith

Ebenezer
1830–1911
m: male issue

ALFRED
1854–1928
m. A. Washington
no male issue

Arthur
1862–1943
m: no male issue

EDWIN
1868–1947
m. H. Kem[

LYDALL
1894–1940
m. (*1*) M. Loscombe (*2*) M. Thorne

ERIC
1895–

by (*1*) JOHN
1917–
m. B. Mence

by (*2*) Timothy
1940–
m. S. Barradale

Jolyon
1958–

Nicholas
1966–

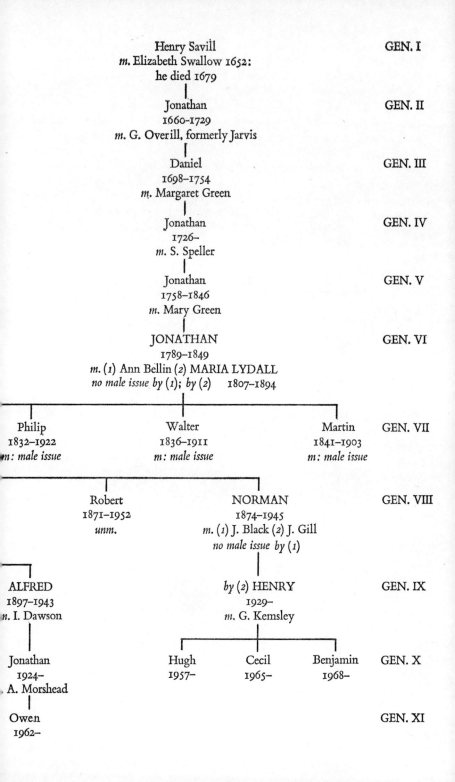

Henry Savill			**GEN. I**
m. Elizabeth Swallow 1652:			
he died 1679			

Jonathan   **GEN. II**
1660–1729
m. G. Overill, formerly Jarvis

Daniel   **GEN. III**
1698–1754
m. Margaret Green

Jonathan   **GEN. IV**
1726–
m. S. Speller

Jonathan   **GEN. V**
1758–1846
m. Mary Green

JONATHAN   **GEN. VI**
1789–1849
m. (1) Ann Bellin (2) MARIA LYDALL
no male issue by (1); by (2)   1807–1894

Philip	Walter	Martin	**GEN. VII**
1832–1922	1836–1911	1841–1903	
m: male issue	*m: male issue*	*m: male issue*	

Robert	NORMAN	**GEN. VIII**
1871–1952	1874–1945	
unm.	m. (1) J. Black (2) J. Gill	
	no male issue by (1)	

ALFRED	by (2) HENRY	**GEN. IX**
1897–1943	1929–	
m. I. Dawson	m. G. Kemsley	

Jonathan	Hugh	Cecil	Benjamin	**GEN. X**
1924–	1957–	1965–	1968–	
m. A. Morshead				

Owen   **GEN. XI**
1962–

Index

of principal persons mentioned in text

Addison, Sir William, 14
Adeane, Charles, 72
Amundsen, Roald, 79
Andrews, Thomas, 80
Arkwright, Rev. Joseph, 40
Arkwright, Loftus, 40
Arkwright, Sir Richard, 40
Asquith, Herbert, 60, 68
Astor, John Jacob, 80
Atkinson, Rev. J. C., 19
Attlee, Clement, 141

Baldwin, Stanley, 122
Balfour, Arthur J., 60
Beesley, Lawrence, 82
Bellin, Samuel, 27, 28
Bismarck, Prince Otto von, 84
Blériot, Louis, 78
Blonfield, Charles James, Bishop
    of London, 26, 165
Bourchier, Frances, 16
Bowers, Lieut. H. R., 79
Bramston, Sir John, 16
Brunel, I. K., 48
Buxton, Sir Thomas Fowell, 52

Campbell-Bannerman, Sir
    Henry, 60
Cave-Bigley, Jacqueline Mary
    (*née* Savill), 107

Chamberlain, Neville, 122-125
Charity, F. W., 129
Christie, A. H., 31, 33
Churchill, Sir Winston, 115,
    122, 151
Clark, Sir Andrew, 150
Clutton, John, 49, 55
Cobbett, William, 19
Connaught, H.R.H. Duke of, 53
Cowdray, Lord, 104
Cromwell, Oliver, 16
Cromwell, Sir Richard, 90
Crouch, R. F., 149

Daniels, Mr, 101
de Soissons, Louis, 91
Dickens, Charles, 23, 57
Douglas-Pennant, H., 156
Dowden, A. J. C., 145, 155
Driver, Edward, 49
Dugdale, Sir Thomas, 149, 150

Edward VII, H.M. King, 74,
    77, 78, 83
Edward VIII, H.M. King, 114,
    122, 123
Elizabeth II, H.M. Queen, 113,
    115
Ernle, Lord, 35, 61, 97

Evans, Helen Cecily (*née* Savill), 75, 76
Evans, Petty Officer Edgar, 79
Eve, George Hubert, 100 *et seq.*, 109, 116, 129, 131, 135
Eve, James George, 45, 109, 129, 131, 138, 148, 150, 156
Eve, Richard, 102, 103
Eve, William, 102
Eve, William Skinner, 102

Featherstone, G. A., 116, 129
Feilden, Cecil, 156
Ferdinand, Archduke Francis, 83
Fisher, W. R., 54

George, V, H.M. King, 83, 112, 122
George VI, H.M. King, 111, 112, 114, 151
George, Henry, 60, 69, 70, 119, 141
Gloucester, H.R.H. Duke of, 116
Goreham, Ambrose, 101, 102
Green, Isaac, 21
Guest, Josiah, 116–118

Harper, Sir Edgar, 69
Harris, A. J., 156
Harsnett, Samuel, Archbishop of York, 23
Heap, Sir Desmond, 14
Heath, Edward, 153, 157
Hitler, Adolf, 123–125, 139
Hobhouse, Sir Arthur, 54
Howard, Sir Ebenezer, 143
Hussey, William, 25

Ireton, Henry, 16
Ives, Leonard, 101

Jarvis, Isaac, 20
Jones, J. H. Emlyn, 145, 154, 155

Kemp, Alexander Davidson, 74, 75
Kemp, Ann, 75
Kent, Nathaniel, 25
Kitchener, Field Marshal Earl, 84

Lakin, Bridget, 14
Lambourne, Lord, 38, 116
Laycock, Peter, 109–111, 126, 129, 132, 138, 154
Lloyd George, David, 60, 64–67, 69, 70
Lockwood, Sir Frank, 39
Lockwood, Lieut.-Col. John, 38, 58
Lockwood, Mark, 38
London, Charles James Blonfield, Bishop of, 26, 165
Long, Henry, 104
Lund, Major-Gen. Otto, 135, 136
Lydall, John, 27
Lydall, Maria, 27

Macdonald, James Ramsay, 122
Maitland, Rev. John Whitaker, 38, 51, 52
Maitland, William Whitaker, 34, 38, 51
Marten, Lieut.-Comdr. George, 148–150
Masham, Sir Hugh, 16

Maslen, Patrick, 154, 155
Mill, John Stuart, 60, 141
Millington, P. W. H., 32
Milner, Viscount, 96

Norden, John, 25
Nugent, G. R. H., 149

Oates, Capt. Laurence, 79

Peacock, Kenneth, 91
Pepys, Samuel, 19
Perry, Rev. George, 34
Phillips, Ritchie, 155
Port, C., 156
Pretyman, Capt. N. G., 65-67

Ragg, Frederick R., 109, 129, 155
Robinson, Newton, 65
Rogers, Julian, 55
Ryde, Edward, 55

Salisbury, Marquess of, 60
Salter, Arthur, 156
Samuel, Herbert, 122
Savill:
  Alfred (1829-1905), 24, 29,
    30-35, 38-40, 42, 43, 46,
    47, 49, 54-61, 64, 74, 87,
    100-103, 115, 137, 154
  Alfred (1854-1928), 60, 74,
    87, 103, 104, 106, 115, 116
  Alfred Cecil (1897-1943),
    74-77, 85, 86, 106, 108, 129,
    132-136, 155
  Alfred Jonathan (b. 1924), 107
  Ann (née Bellin), 27
  Arthur Edward (1862-1943),
    56, 74, 75

  Augusta (née Washington), 74
  Benjamin Edward (b. 1968),
    155
  Betty Constance (née Mence),
    139
  Cecil Henry (b. 1965), 155
  Daniel (1698-1754), 18, 21
  Daniel (1771-1828), 22
  Ebenezer (1830-1911), 29, 107
  Edwin Lydall (1894-1940),
    74-77, 84, 85, 87, 100, 106,
    109, 126, 129, 132, 138
  Edwin, Sir (1868-1947), 32,
    40, 56, 60 et seq., 61, 66,
    67, 71, 72, 74-77, 87-89,
    92-94, 96, 98, 100, 104,
    106-111, 115, 129, 132,
    137, 138, 145, 154, 155
  Eleanor (née Hallings Smith),
    31, 55, 56, 57, 74
  Elizabeth (ne Swallow),
    15-20, 137, 164
  Eric Humphrey, Sir (b. 1895),
    58, 75-77, 84, 85, 100,
    106, 109, 111-114
  Gillian (née Kemsley), 155
  Grace (formerly Overhill, née
    Jarvis), 20, 21
  Helen (née Kemp), 74-77, 112
  Helen Cecily, 75, 76
  Henry (d. 1679), 15-20, 137,
    164
  Henry Edward (b. 1929),
    118, 138, 151, 155
  Henry Norman (1874-1945),
    56, 60, 74, 87, 100, 106,
    111, 115, 116, 118, 129,
    137, 138, 158
  Irene (née Dawson), 107

Savill—*cont.*
  Isaac (1774–1862), 22
  Jacqueline Mary, 107
  Jane (*née* Black), 74, 118
  Jean (*née* Gill), 118, 155
  John Loscombe Lydall
    (b. 1917), 106, 137–139
  Jolyon Robert Lydall
    (b. 1958), 139
  Jonathan (1660–1729), 18, 20,
    21
  Jonathan (1726–?), 21
  Jonathan (1758–1846), 15, 22,
    23, 26, 27
  Jonathan (1789–1849), 24, 28,
    29, 31, 32, 36, 37, 61, 154,
    165
  Joseph (1798–1876), 56
  Lambert (1656–1729), 18
  Marjorie (*née* Loscombe), 106,
    132
  Margaret (*née* Green), 21
  Margaret (*née* Thorne), 132
  Maria (*née* Lydall), 27–31, 75
  Martha (*née* Felton), 21
  Martin (1841–1903), 29, 30,
    56
  Mary (*née* Green), 22
  Norman Hugh (b. 1957), 155
  Philip (1832–1922), 29, 56
  Robert Cecil (1871–1952),
    56, 74, 137
  Sarah (*née* Speller), 21
  Sidney (1848–1861), 29
  Sidney Rowland (1891–1967),
    107
  Timothy Lydall (b. 1940), 132
  Walter (1836–1911), 29, 30,
    57

Saxton, Christopher, 25
Scott, Capt. Robert Falcon, 78,
  79
Shakeshaft, Thomas and Ann,
  18
Shaw, Richard Norman, 57
Shaw, Robert Ewart, 30, 57
Shores, Charles, 129
Smith, Edward J., FRICS, 14
Smith, Capt. Edward J., MN,
  80
Smith, R. C., 100, 101
Smith, Sir Thomas, 19
Speed, John, 25
Spencer-Churchill, Capt.
  Edward, 45
Steer, Francis, 17
Stephenson, George, 47
Stourton, M. G. P., 156

Thompson, F. M. L., 14
Turner, Alexander W., 109,
  129, 138, 156

Veale, Pte Theodore Henry,
  85
Victoria, H.M. Queen, 39,
  53–55, 58, 59, 61, 64, 77

Watson, John A. F., 120, 121,
  137, 144–147, 154, 155
Webster, H. R. J., 91, 154, 156
White, D. E., 139
William II, Emperor of
  Germany (the Kaiser), 84
Willingale, Samuel, 52
Willingale, Thomas, 52
Willis, Henry W., 29
Wilson Dr E. R., 79

Wilson, Sir Harold, 153, 157

Wilson, J. C., 156

Wimborne, Viscount, 115–118, 129

Wright, Richard, 18

York, Samuel Harsnett, Archbishop of, 23